Academic Language Mastery

Volumes in the
Academic Language Mastery Series

Series Editor: Ivannia Soto

Academic Language Mastery: Grammar and Syntax in Context
David E. Freeman, Yvonne S. Freeman, and Ivannia Soto

Academic Language Mastery: Conversational Discourse in Context
Jeff Zwiers and Ivannia Soto

Academic Language Mastery: Vocabulary in Context
Margarita Calderón and Ivannia Soto

Academic Language Mastery: Culture in Context
Noma LeMoine and Ivannia Soto

Academic Language Mastery:
Culture
in Context

Noma LeMoine
Ivannia Soto

CORWIN
A SAGE Publishing Company

A SAGE Publishing Company

FOR INFORMATION:

Corwin

A SAGE Company

2455 Teller Road

Thousand Oaks, California 91320

(800) 233-9936

www.corwin.com

SAGE Publications Ltd.

1 Oliver's Yard

55 City Road

London EC1Y 1SP

United Kingdom

SAGE Publications India Pvt. Ltd.

B 1/I 1 Mohan Cooperative Industrial Area

Mathura Road, New Delhi 110 044

India

SAGE Publications Asia-Pacific Pte. Ltd.

3 Church Street

#10-04 Samsung Hub

Singapore 049483

Program Director: Dan Alpert

Senior Associate Editor: Kimberly Greenberg

Editorial Assistant: Katie Crilley

Production Editor: Amy Schroller

Copy Editor: Pam Schroeder

Typesetter: C&M Digitals (P) Ltd.

Proofreader: Dennis W. Webb

Indexer: Sheia Bodell

Cover Designer: Anupama Krishnan

Marketing Manager: Charline Maher

Printed in the United States of America

ISBN 978-1-5063-3715-9

This book is printed on acid-free paper.

SUSTAINABLE FORESTRY INITIATIVE

Certified Chain of Custody
Promoting Sustainable Forestry
www.sfiprogram.org
SFI-01268

SFI label applies to text stock

16 17 18 19 20 10 9 8 7 6 5 4 3 2 1

Contents

Acknowledgments

I would like to acknowledge each of the authors who coauthored this series with me: Margarita Calderón, David and Yvonne Freeman, Noma LeMoine, and Jeff Zwiers. I have been inspired by each of your work for so long, and it was an honor learning and working with you on this project. I know that this book series is stronger due to each of your contributions, and will therefore affect the lives of so many English language learners (ELLs) and standard English learners (SELs). Thank you for taking this journey with me on behalf of students who need our collective voices!

I would also like to acknowledge my editor, Dan Alpert, who has believed in me and has supported my work since 2008. Thank you for tirelessly advocating for equity, including language equity, for so long! Thank you also for advocating for and believing in the vision of the Institute for Culturally and Linguistically Responsive Teaching (ICLRT)!

Also to be thanked is Corwin, for supporting my work over time as well as early contributions to ICLRT. Corwin has grown over the time that I published my first book in 2009, but they still remain a family. I would especially like to thank Michael Soule, Lisa Shaw, Kristin Anderson, Monique Corrdiori, Amelia Arias, Taryn Waters, Charline Maher, Kim Greenberg, and Katie Crilley for each of your parts in making this book series and ICLRT a success!

Last, I would like to acknowledge the California Community Foundation, whose two-year grant assisted greatly with fully launching ICLRT at Whittier College. Thank you for believing that effective professional development over time can and will create achievement and life changes for ELLs and SELs!

PUBLISHER'S ACKNOWLEDGMENTS

Corwin gratefully acknowledges the contributions of the following reviewers:

Delores B. Lindsey
Professor, Education Leadership, retired
California State University San Marcos
Escondido, CA

Randall Lindsey
Emeritus Professor
California State University, Los Angeles
Escondido, CA

Katherine Lobo
ESL Teacher and Teacher Trainer
Newton Public Schools and Brandeis University
Arlington, MA

Ray Terrell
Education Professor
Miami University
Oxford, OH

About the Authors

Dr. Noma LeMoine has served more than 10 years as adjunct professor at several California universities and colleges. Her research interests and expertise include language and literacy acquisition in SEL populations, methodologies for improving learning in culturally and linguistically diverse student populations, and the impact of teacher training on classroom instruction. Dr. LeMoine writes curriculum; designs and conducts professional development for teachers, administrators, paraeducators, and parents; and consults with institutions of higher learning and K–12 schools relative to advancing learning in traditionally underachieving students. She has conducted seminars and been guest lecturer at school districts throughout North America and at colleges and universities including Harvard, Dartmouth, Stanford, University of Southern California, University of Minnesota, University of Massachusetts Amherst, University of California, Berkeley, and University of California, Los Angeles. Dr. LeMoine has served on education committees including the California State Department of Education's Exemplary Schools Committee and University Accreditation Team and the National Citizens Commission on African American Education, an arm of the Congressional Black Caucus Education Brain Trust. Her work has taken her on educational tours and exchanges to the Caribbean, Africa, India, and China.

Dr. LeMoine has received professional honors and awards including the California Speech-Language-Hearing Association Outstanding Achievement Award (1988), and the Lois V. Douglass Distinguished Alumnus Award, from the Department of Communication Disorders at California State University, Los Angeles. In April 1992, Dr. LeMoine was named Fellow of the California Speech-Language-Hearing Association. Mount St. Mary's

College awarded Dr. LeMoine the Cultural Fluency Award in 1997 in recognition of outstanding contributions to the development of cross-cultural understanding in the Los Angeles community. In June 2005, the Association of California School Administrators bestowed upon Dr. LeMoine the Region XVI Valuing Diversity Award for her work in Los Angeles Unified School District toward closing the achievement gap. In February 2008, the Southern California Chapter of the California Alliance of African American Educators bestowed upon Dr. LeMoine the Asa G. Hilliard III Will to Educate Award for distinguished service on behalf of African American students, and in November 2009, Dr. LeMoine received the Distinguished Educator Award from the Southern California Affiliate of the National Council of Negro Women.

 **Dr. Ivannia Soto** is associate professor of education at Whittier College, where she specializes in second language acquisition, systemic reform for ELLs, and urban education. She began her career in the Los Angeles Unified School District (LAUSD), where she taught English and English language development to a population made up of 99.9 percent Latinos, who either were or had been ELLs. Before becoming a professor, Dr. Soto also served LAUSD as a literacy coach and district office administrator. She has presented on literacy and language topics at various conferences, including the National Association for Bilingual Education (NABE), the California Association for Bilingual Education (CABE), the American Educational Research Association (AERA), and the National Urban Education Conference. As a consultant, Soto has worked with Stanford University's School Redesign Network (SRN) and WestEd as well as a variety of districts and county offices in California, providing technical assistance for systemic reform for ELLs and Title III. Soto is the coauthor of *The Literacy Gaps: Building Bridges for ELLs and SELs* as well as author of *ELL Shadowing as a Catalyst for Change* and *From Spoken to Written Language With ELLs*, all published by Corwin. Together, the books tell a story of how to systemically close achievement gaps with ELLs by increasing their oral language production in academic areas.

Soto is executive director of the Institute for Culturally and Linguistically Responsive Teaching (ICLRT) at Whittier College, whose mission it is to promote relevant research and develop academic resources for ELLs and SELs via linguistically and culturally responsive teaching practices.

Series Dedication

I dedicate this book series to the teachers and administrators in Whittier Union High School District (WUHSD). WUHSD has been a pivotal learning partner with ICLRT over the past four years. By embedding ICLRT Design Principles and academic language development (ALD) best practices into their teaching and professional development, they have fully embraced and worked tirelessly in classrooms to meet the needs of ELLs and SELs. Specifically, I would like to thank: Superintendent Sandy Thorstenson, Assistant Superintendent Loring Davies, and ELL Director Lilia Torres-Cooper (my high school counselor and the person who initially brought me into WUHSD) as well as ALD Certification teachers Diana Banzet, Amy Cantrell, Carlos Contreras, Carmen Telles Fox, Nellie Garcia, Kristin Kowalsky, Kelsey McDonnell, Damian Torres, and Heather Vernon, who have committed themselves fully to this work. I would also like to thank Lori Eshilian, principal of Whittier High School (my high school alma mater), for being willing to do whatever it takes to meet the needs of all students, including partnering with ICLRT on several projects over the past few years. You were my first and best physical education teacher and have modeled effective collaboration since I was in high school!

—Ivannia Soto, Series Editor

Book Dedication

This book is dedicated to my dad, Howell Bunton,
who assured me I could do anything I put my mind to,
to my mom, Maggie Bunton,
who gave me the spiritual acumen to do just that,
to my son, Armand LeMoyne,
who is the absolute love of my life, and
to great teachers everywhere
who invest their time, energy, and heart into children's lives.

—Noma LeMoine

CHAPTER ONE

Introduction to the Book Series

According to the Migration Policy Institute (2013), close to 5 million U.S. students, which represent 9 percent of public school enrollment, are English language learners (ELLs). Three-quarters of these 5 million students were born in the United States and are either the children or grandchildren of immigrants. In some large urban school districts such as Los Angeles, ELLs already comprise around 30 percent of the student population. These demographic trends, along with the rigorous content expectations of new content and language standards (e.g., CCSS, WIDA, ELPA21, etc.), require that educational systems become skilled at simultaneously scaffolding academic language and content for this growing group of students. For ELLs, academic language mastery is the key to accessing rigorous content. Now is a pivotal time in educational history to address both academic language and content simultaneously so that ELLs do not fall further behind in both areas while also becoming bored by methods that are cognitively banal and lead to disengagement.

Another group of students who have academic language needs, but are not formally identified as such, are standard English learners (SELs). SELs are students who speak languages that do not correspond to standard American English language structure and grammar but incorporate English vocabulary. They include African American students who speak African American language (AAL), sometimes referred to as African American English, and Mexican

American–non-new-immigrant students who speak Mexican American Language (MxAL) or what is commonly referred to as "Chicano English." Both ELLs and SELs need instructional assistance in the academic language necessary to be successful in school, college, and beyond. For both groups of students, academic language represents the pathway to full access in meeting the rigorous demands of the new standards.

Purpose of This Academic Language Development Book Series

The purpose of this series is to assist educators in developing expertise in, and practical strategies for, addressing four key dimensions of academic language when working with ELLs and SELs. To systemically address the needs of ELLs and SELs, we educators must share a common understanding of academic language development (ALD). Wong-Fillmore (2013) defines academic language as "the language of texts. The forms of speech and written discourse that are linguistic resources educated people in our society can draw on. This is language that is capable of supporting complex thought, argumentation, literacy, successful learning; it is the language used in written and spoken communication in college and beyond" (p. 15). Given that we are preparing ELLs and SELs for college, career, and beyond, they should receive ample opportunities to learn and use academic language, both in spoken and written form (Soto, 2014). ELLs and SELs also must be provided with scaffolded access to cognitively and linguistically demanding content, which allows them to cultivate their complex thinking and argumentation.

All students can benefit from academic language development modeling, scaffolding, and practice, but ELLs and SELs need it to survive and thrive in school. ELLs have plenty of language assets in their primary language that we must leverage to grow their academic English, yet there is often a very clear language and literacy gap that must be closed as soon as ELLs enter school. Similarly, SELs come to school with a language variation that, to be built upon in the classroom setting, must first be understood. In reviewing the wide range of literature by experts in this field, most agree that the key elements of academic English language for ELLs and SELs include these four dimensions: academic vocabulary, syntax and grammar, discourse, and culturally responsive teaching.

We have therefore organized this book series around these four dimensions of academic English:

- Conversational Discourse—developing students' conversational skills as an avenue for fostering academic language and thinking in a discipline
- Academic Vocabulary—teaching high-frequency academic words and discipline-specific vocabulary across content areas
- Syntax and Grammar—teaching sophisticated and complex syntactical and grammatical structures in context
- Culturally Responsive Teaching—incorporating culture while addressing and teaching language, and honoring students' home cultures and communities

The focus on these four dimensions in this book series makes this a unique offering for educators. By building upon the cultural and linguistic similarities of ELLs and SELs, we embed strategies and instructional approaches about academic vocabulary, discourse, and grammar and syntax within culturally responsive teaching practices, to make them all accessible to teachers of diverse students. As the American poet and great thinker of modern Hispanic literature, Sabine Ulibarrí, noted, "Language is culture; it carries with it traditions, customs, the very life of a people. You cannot separate one from the other. To love one is to love the other; to hate one is to hate the other. If one wants to destroy a people, take away their language and their culture will soon disappear." Therefore, the heart of this book series is to integrate language and culture in a manner that has not been addressed with other books or book series on ALD.

ACADEMIC LANGUAGE DEVELOPMENT DIMENSIONS DEFINED AND CONNECTIONS TO THE BOOK SERIES

ALD is a pathway to equity. With new rigorous state standards and expectations, ALD is the scaffold that provides access for ELLs and SELs so that high academic expectations can be maintained and reached. The following matrix defines each dimension of ALD and demonstrates the intersection of ALD dimensions across the book series. For full proficiency in ALD, it is integral that each dimension be addressed across disciplines—the dimensions should not be taught as either/or skills. Instead, each of the dimensions should be addressed throughout a course of study or unit. In that way, it is important to read the book series in its entirety, as an ongoing professional development growth tool (more on that later). The matrix also demonstrates the connections made between ALD dimensions, which will prove helpful as readers complete continue their study across the ALD book series.

ALD Dimension	Definition	Connections to the Book Series
Academic Discourse	Academic discourse is putting words and sentences (the other two dimensions) together to clearly communicate complex ideas. The essential components of academic discourse include: • Message organization and text structure • Voice and register • Density of words, sentences, and ideas • Clarity and coherence • Purpose, functions, and audience	As suggested in the definition, academic discourse involves the overlap of academic vocabulary (words) and many of the components also often associated with academic writing across genres (organization, text structure, purpose, and audience). This book addresses a specific form of discourse, conversational discourse, and the specific conversational skills that provide access to academic discourse.
Academic Vocabulary	Words are separate units of information; it is tempting to focus on them as "pieces of knowledge" to accumulate to show learning. Instead, words should be tools and materials for constructing more complete and complex messages. In this book series, we will focus on Tier 2 (high-frequency words that go across content areas) and Tier 3 (abstract or nuanced words that exist within a particular content area or discipline) academic vocabulary.	Academic vocabulary is associated with the density of words used in academic discourse as well as the use of connectives and transitions used in grammar.

ALD Dimension	Definition	Connections to the Book Series
Grammar and Syntax in Context	Academic language is characterized by technical vocabulary, lexical density, and abstraction. Academic genres have predictable components, cohesive texts, and language structures that include nominalizations, passives, and complex sentences.	ELLs and SELs need to engage in academic discourse in the classroom and develop academic vocabulary. These are essential building blocks for learning to read and write cohesive texts using academic genres and the language structures characteristic of academic language.
Culturally and Linguistically Responsive Practices	Culturally responsive pedagogy incorporates high-status, accurate cultural knowledge about different ethnic groups into all subjects and skills taught. It validates, facilitates, liberates, and empowers ethnically diverse students by simultaneously cultivating their cultural integrity, individual abilities, and academic success (Gay, 2000).	ELLs and SELs are more likely to acquire ALD when they are viewed from an asset model and when ALD is taught as associated with concepts that connect to their cultural knowledge. This book will address linguistic diversity, including variations of English.

(Definitions adapted from Academic Language Development Network (n.d.) unless otherwise noted)

FORMAT FOR EACH BOOK

At the beginning of each book is an introduction to the purpose of the book series and the need for ALD across content areas. Additionally, connections between current ALD research and the specific dimension of ALD are included in an abbreviated literature review as well as connections to specific ICLRT Design Principles. In the middle of each book, the voice of the expert in the particular ALD dimension is incorporated. These chapters include how to move from theory to practice, classroom examples at elementary and secondary levels, and ways to assess the dimension. At the end of each book, a summary of major points and how to overcome related challenges along with the rationale for use of the Institute for

Culturally and Linguistically Responsive Teaching (ICLRT) Design Principles as a bridge between ALD and content.

Additionally, each book in the series is organized in a similar manner for ease of use by the reader. Chapter 1 is the introduction to the series of books and not an introduction for each individual book. Instead, Chapter 2 introduces each dimension of ALD with the specific research base for that book. The heart of each book in the series is in Chapter 3, where practical application to theory and classroom examples can be found. Chapter 4 addresses how each ALD dimension fosters literacy development. In Chapter 5, how to assess the specific ALD dimension is discussed with checklists and rubrics to assist with formative assessment in this area. Last, Chapter 6 connects each volume with the others in the series and details how the book series can best be used in a professional development setting. The epilogue revisits the vision for the series and provides a description of the relationship to the underlying principles of ICLRT.

- Chapter 1—Introduction to the Book Series
- Chapter 2—Abbreviated Literature Review: The Case for Culturally Relevant and Linguistically Responsive Pedagogy
- Chapter 3—Practical Application: Culturally and Linguistically Responsive Instructional Strategies That Advance Learning in EL and SEL Populations
- Chapter 4—Fostering Literacy With CLRP
- Chapter 5—Assessing for Culturally and Linguistically Responsive Indicators
- Chapter 6—Conclusions, Challenges, and Connections
- Epilogue: The Vision

How to Use the Book Series

While each book can stand alone, the book series was designed to be read together with colleagues and over time. As such, it is a professional development tool for educational communities, which can also be used for extended learning on ALD. Educators may choose to begin with any of the four key dimensions of ALD that interests them the most or with which they need the most assistance.

HOW TO USE REFLECT AND APPLY QUERIES

Embedded throughout this book series you will find queries that will ask you to reflect and apply new learning to your own practice. Please note that you may choose to use the queries in a variety of settings either with a book study buddy during PLC, grade-level, or department meetings. Each of the queries can be answered in a separate journal while one is reading the text, or as a group you may choose to reflect on only a few queries throughout a chapter. Please feel free to use as many or as few queries as are helpful to you, but we do encourage you to at least try a couple out for reflection as you read the book series.

Try it out by responding to the first query here.

REFLECT AND APPLY

What does the Sabine Ulibarrí quote below mean to you? How does it connect to your students?

"Language is culture; it carries with it traditions, customs, the very life of a people. You cannot separate one from the other. To love one is to love the other; to hate one is to hate the other. If one wants to destroy a people, take away their language and their culture will soon disappear."

BOOK SERIES CONNECTION TO CULTURALLY AND LINGUISTICALLY RESPONSIVE TEACHING

Culturally and linguistically responsive teaching is an essential dimension of ALD. Often, however, educators may be reluctant to make space for culturally and/or linguistically responsive teaching as that is not the way that they were taught. In an increasingly pluralistic society, it is essential that we teach the student in front of us and not the student that we might have been. By teaching in a culturally and linguistically responsive manner, we are allowing students from culturally and linguistically diverse backgrounds to see themselves represented in school, which will be both motivating and engaging for them. It is definitely worth the effort to invest in getting to know the cultural and linguistic histories of the students that we teach, as the payoff in the end can be dramatic.

Some educators may struggle with how to meet the cultural and linguistic needs of their students, as they may have many more questions than solutions. Investing in book studies and professional development on teaching diverse populations of students will prove helpful, as it may not be a natural skill to provide instruction from that lens. Having a support team or group of teachers who also value, or are in the process of acquiring, cultural and linguistic teaching skills can be helpful as together you can jointly take instructional risks.

Still other educators may struggle with having what Glenn Singleton calls "courageous conversations about race." Perhaps you have felt uncomfortable with discussing culture as you do not want to inadvertently hurt someone or demonstrate inexperience about the topic. It is important to note that whether we are educators of color or not, we all must be in process when it comes to having difficult or courageous conversations about race, culture, or language and how these apply to the students we are teaching. Everybody comes to teaching with their own values and biases, which are framed from personal experiences, and can grow in the area of culturally and linguistically responsive teaching. Educators of color may realize that socioeconomically and linguistically, they are now much different than the students they teach, and they may need to remind themselves of the financial and language struggle once again. This book in the series is an opportunity for educators to do just that: take the risk to meet both the language *and* cultural needs of their students with an equity focus.

CHAPTER TWO

Abbreviated Literature Review

The Case for Culturally Relevant and Linguistically Responsive Pedagogy

"A child cannot be taught by anyone whose demand, essentially, is that the child repudiate his experience and all that gives him sustenance." —James Baldwin (1979)

The cultural and linguistic diversity of ELLs and SELs who populate the large, urban cities of America creates significant educational challenges for educators. Language and cultural differences in ELL and SEL students, and how teachers perceive and respond to those differences, are key variables impacting diverse students' access to core curricula, to college preparatory course work, to postsecondary educational opportunities, and to career success. Negative attitudes toward the language and culture of ELL and SEL students shape, to a significant degree, the educational and instructional practices that often result in denial of opportunities to learn at high levels. Teachers with a good understanding of the language, learning styles, and cultural strengths ELL and SEL students bring to the classroom, are in a much better position to positively impact their learning. The more knowledge they have about the language and culture of English learner (EL) and SEL populations, the more positive their attitude is toward the students as learners and the greater their willingness to negotiate identities in the class-room to facilitate learning (LeMoine, 2003).

WHAT IS CULTURALLY AND LINGUISTICALLY RESPONSIVE TEACHING (CLRT)?

Geneva Gay (2000) provides one of the most definitive definitions of culturally responsive pedagogy; she writes

> Culturally responsive pedagogy . . . uses ways of knowing, understanding, and representing various ethnic groups in teaching academic subjects, processes, and skills. It culti-vates cooperation, collaboration, reciprocity, and mutual responsibility for learning among students and between students and teachers. It incorporates high-status, accurate cultural knowledge about different ethnic groups into all subjects and skills taught. . . . [It] validates, facilitates, liber-ates, and empowers ethnically diverse students by simulta-neously cultivating their cultural integrity, individual abilities, and academic success. (pp. 43–44)

We draw upon Gay's definition in this text and additionally consider it essential to highlight the importance of incorporating "accurate linguistic knowledge" about different ethnic groups into the curricu-lum and cultivating students' "linguistic integrity" as a means of academic empowerment.

The culture and language a student brings to the classroom matters and has vast implications for how the learning environ-ment should be structured if learning is to occur. "Culture is to humans as water is to fish," Nobles (2015) asserts, inferring its all-encompassing nature. It is, he contends, "the invisible medium in which all human functioning occurs," thus it cannot be sepa-rated from the educational environment or the curriculum. According to the research, when we incorporate into instruction the cultural referents that influence the social practices of stu-dents, the result is enhanced academic performance (Bailey & Boykin, 2001; Boykin & Cunningham, 2001; Gay, 2000; Ladson-Billings, 2009). Culturally and linguistically responsive pedagogy

(CLRP) maximizes learning for diverse students, including ELs and SELs. CLRP acknowledges the importance of including students' cultural referents in all aspects of the learning experience and increases learning opportunities by making critical connections to who students are and to their history, culture, language, prior knowledge, experiences, and learning styles and, by using that knowledge, to bridge new learning experiences.

WHAT THE RESEARCH SAYS AND WHY CLRT MATTERS IN THE EDUCATION OF ELs AND SELs

According to the research, cultural discontinuities can and do exist in classrooms in language, cognitive learning styles, work habits, and problem solving (Boykin, 2001; Delpit, 2006; Gay, 2000; Hollins & Oliver, 1999; Ladson-Billings, 2009), and these gaps can represent significant hurdles to successful teaching and learning in culturally and linguistically diverse classrooms. Cultural discontinuity is defined as a cultural disconnection between students' home environments and that of the school (Boykin, 2001). Differences in the functional use of language have been found to account for a large percentage of this discontinuity. All too often the languages of ELs and SELs are delegitimized in instruction, with the languages of SELs regularly viewed as aberrant or as corruptions of the dominant language. The cultural experiences, prior knowledge, and learning and interacting styles of culturally and linguistically diverse students are viewed as deviant, and many teachers believe it is their job to purge diverse students of any traces of their culture and language.

There is consensus in the research that CLRP is an effective antidote for the incongruence experienced by diverse learners in the classroom (Cummins, 2001; Delpit & Dowdy, 2002; Gay, 2000). According to Ladson-Billings (2009), "It transcends the negative effects on diverse students of not seeing their history, culture or background represented in textbooks or curriculum and it allows them to choose academic excellence yet still identify positively with their culture" (p. 17). Studies show that when minority students have positive attitudes toward both their own culture and the dominant culture, school failure does not occur (Cummins, 2001). Ladson-Billings (2009) reports that teachers who practice culturally relevant teaching know how to support learning in diverse students (ELs and SELs) by consciously creating social interactions to help them meet the criteria of academic success, cultural competence, and critical consciousness. These teachers, Ladson-Billings asserts, demonstrate a connectedness with students, develop a community of learners rather than competitive individual achievement, and encourage students to learn collaboratively, teach each other, and be responsible for each other's success. Teachers who develop culturally consistent ways of interacting with students from different cultures adapt instruction so that diverse learners feel accepted and affirmed in the classroom.

Every child deserves a competent, qualified teacher, one who has the capacity to transform the classroom into a safe place where all students are accepted and affirmed and where genuine relationships are built, seeds of knowledge are planted, minds are awakened, and lives are transformed. Learning occurs in social environments and is heavily influenced by the cultural experiences, linguistic proficiencies, and funds of knowledge both students and teachers bring to the learning environment, and when there is alignment between students' cultural experiences and the culture and language of school, learning is accelerated (Cummins, 2001; Gay, 2000; Ladson-Billings, 2009). Because an individual's culture and language are central to his or her existence, it is virtually impossible to separate the influence of culture from the learning experience. Gay (2000) corroborates this assertion; she states, "When instructional processes are consistent with the cultural orientations, experiences, and learning styles of marginalized . . . students, their school achievement improves significantly" (p. 181). Baldwin (1979) agrees; he says, "A child cannot be taught by anyone whose demand, essentially, is that the child repudiate his experience and all that gives him sustenance." For ELs and SELs this interrelationship of culture and learning infers instruction that validates and accommodates the home language and culture in the acquisition of school language and literacy and thus affirms CLRT as appropriate pedagogy.

Traditional instructional approaches may not provide the same benefits for ELL and SEL students as it does for their more "mainstream" peers. They may experience barriers to accessing core curricula because of the culture and language differences they bring to the learning environment. The research supports the contention that students are able to access core curricula more easily when their culture and language matches the language of school (Cummins, 2001; Irvine & Armento, 2001), thus assuring equity in opportunities to learn. Increasing academic achievement in ELs and SELs will require more culturally relevant and linguistically responsive methods of instruction.

The concept of "culturally responsive" teaching is not new. Traditional education in America has always been culturally responsive, although primarily to middle class Europeans; it makes critical connections to European history, culture, and language, to their canons of literature, learning styles, and their life experiences which are infused into the very fabric of instruction. Indeed if we need validation that CLRP works, we need only look at the effectiveness of America's educational institutions with the population whose needs it was originally designed to address. However, America has now opened the doors of education to all of its residents, and for some students, the Eurocentric paradigm for teaching and learning is not a good fit. Culturally and linguistically diverse students who bring different cultural experiences, histories, languages, and canons of literature are not always well served in European-centered learning environments, where their culture, language, and experiences are devalued or viewed through deficit lenses. Gay (2000) contends "cultural variables" often explain school failure in diverse student populations. EL and SEL students' academic performance is frequently viewed apart from their culture, language, ethnicity, and personal experiences and is decontextualized in ways that do not serve them well in the learning environment. EL and SEL students whose home and community environments differ from the Eurocentric norms of American schools may, because of the "culture-specific" ways in which they were socialized, display language and behaviors that are different from their more mainstream peers and may acquire knowledge and demonstrate learning in diverse ways. As educators it is our responsibility to assure the efficacy of the learning experience, thus we have an obligation to better the congruence between the culture of school and the cultures of our ELL and SEL students.

Incorporating elements of diverse students' cultures and life experiences into the learning environment will help affirm diverse students as members of the learning community and acknowledge their contribution to the learning process.

WHO ARE SELS?

"There is no reason to believe that any nonstandard vernacular is itself an obstacle to learning. The chief problem is ignorance of language on the part of all concerned."

—William Labov (1972)

All too often teachers lack even rudimentary knowledge about the cultural and linguistic histories of SEL populations and about methodologies for helping them acquire the culture, language, and literacies of school. SELs are one of the most overlooked, misunderstood, and underserved language-different populations in American educational institutions. It is for this reason that a brief discussion about SEL populations is provided. It is hoped that this overview will help teachers gain a better understanding of the language and learning needs of our SEL populations.

SELs are part of a larger language minority population that can be referred to as standard language learners or those students for whom the standard language—that is, the standard language of the dominate group in the society and thus of its institutions—is not native. The standard language, for example "Standard American English," "Standard Australian English," or "Standard Canadian English," is not the language intuited by the standard language learner in the first four to five years of life. The languages they acquire in the home during the early language acquisition period from their primary care giver are languages that incorporate the vocabulary of the dominant language group, but have maintained much of the structure and form (grammars) of their respective indigenous languages.

The SEL populations whose needs are addressed in this text include African American speakers of "African American language," a language referred to in the research by many names and that has its linguistic base in indigenous West African, specifically Niger Congo, languages; Native Indian speakers of "American Indian language," often referred to as "American Indian English" (Leap 1993), and which is heavily influenced by ancestral American Indian languages; Hawaiian American speakers of "Hawaiian American language," sometimes referred to as "Hawaiian Pidgin English," which draws a considerable amount of its grammatical structure from indigenous Hawaiian languages; and Mexican American speakers of "Mexican American Language" also known as "Chicano English," which is based grammatically in Spanish. None of the SEL groups delineated here were indigenous speakers of English, but as a result of contact with English-speaking populations, their languages were re-lexified with vocabulary (lexical) borrowings from English, creating new languages that incorporate English vocabulary but do not mirror "Standard English" grammar.

The acquisition of language in children is a species-specific phenomenon; as humans we have a biological predisposition to acquire an oral-spoken communication system unique to us as a species. All normally developing human children have this innate propensity to acquire language and, by the age of four or five, have mastered the language of the home or primary caregiver. SELs are no exception. Although the language of their home may differ from the language of school in form and structure, SELs are not deficient language learners; they have successfully accomplished the task of intuiting complex linguistic rules from a model and perfectly matching that model in how they construct and generate language. For the SEL this means the child's language mastery or "linguistic competence" is in a language other than standard American or academic English and therefore does not match the language of school or meet teacher expectation. Because English lexicon (vocabulary) predominates their languages, they are considered "English only" students. The English vocabulary they have in common with "standard English speakers" effectively veils the significant differences in structure and grammar that characterize the languages of SELs and that are traceable to indigenous language grammars. These linguistic differences are often viewed through a deficit lens and perceived of as language deficiencies as opposed to language differences. This incorrect view of SELs as students in need of language remediation instead of second language acquisition has resulted in the widening of proficiency gaps between SELs and their monolingual standard English-speaking peers.

Quality teaching for SELs and ELs will require more than mastery of the academic content to deliver effective instruction in the classroom. Effective teaching of SELs will require educators to increase their knowledge and awareness of the cultural and linguistic capital these students bring to the learning environment, and it will necessitate developing caring relationships, making connections to their prior knowledge and experiences, and fostering positive beliefs relative to their ability to learn at high levels. Educators must draw upon instructional pedagogy that builds on the unique cultural and linguistic background of EL and SEL students and use that knowledge to scaffold access to rigorous college preparatory curricula. Failure to accommodate the culture and language of our EL and SEL students in instruction in culturally and linguistically responsive ways will result in minimal opportunities for these students to meaningfully engage with content area knowledge.

CLRT AND DIVERGENCE IN LEARNING STYLES

The research on learning styles extends at least four decades. How students learn, the methods they use, and the resulting outcomes are important dynamics in the classroom that significantly impact instruction. Important questions in the learning-style research are how to explain variation in learning outcomes for different students and whether learning style theory is an effective pedagogical basis for making instructional decisions. The position taken in this text is that ELs and SELs do bring different cultural orientations to the task of learning, and how they process information and construct knowledge may differ from their more mainstream peers. Their cognitive, communication, interaction, and response styles are often at variance with traditional, European-centered styles of processing information that is often viewed as normative in American educational institutions.

Learning styles have been defined as "characteristic cognitive, affective, and physiological behaviors that serve as relatively stable indicators of how learners perceive, interact, and respond to the learning environment" (O'Neil, 1990). Much of the research affirms that cultural and ethnic groups have distinct ways of processing information, interacting, communicating, and learning (Gay 2000; Ladson-Billings, 2009; Pritchard, 2014). Although there have been many recent challenges to learning style theory, this text takes the position that it is axiomatic that humans, consciously or subconsciously, apply their cognitive styles (their characteristic approaches to perceiving, thinking, and solving problems) to learning situations and that one's cognitive style is very closely aligned with how one is socialized culturally. Thus, if ELs and SLs are to benefit from traditional American school experiences, their cognitive, communication, and interaction styles must be considered in designing instruction.

Palmer (2007) suggests that the best way to teach a student is in the way that he or she learns. It is important that traditional public schools acknowledge and affirm the cultural, linguistic, and learning style differences EL and SEL students bring to the learning environment and that teachers are able to contextualize instruction in the ways these students learn. When teachers fail to consider cultural learning styles in their instructional design, it can create major barriers to learning, and if these barriers to accessing core curricula are to be removed, and the high rate of failure experienced by ELs and SELs in traditional classrooms reversed, instruction must accommodate cultural learning style differences. However, the best way to address these concerns may not be in attempting to build instruction around students' individual learning styles; it is suggested herein that multiple-modality approaches to instruction—the presentation of new material in many different ways—take precedence over the traditional single-modality method of teaching when instructing ELs and SELs. Teachers who incorporate multiple-modality instructional approaches increase the likelihood that the modes of instruction most culturally compatible with SEL and ELL students will be accessible to them and learning facilitated.

Ladson-Billings (2009) suggests that culturally responsive teaching is a pedagogy that "empowers students intellectually, socially, emotionally, and politically by using cultural referents to impart knowledge, skills, and attitudes" (p. 20). To assure equity for all students in accessing rigorous core curricula, we must examine the instructional methodologies and pedagogies utilized in the classroom and other learning environments relative to whether or not they are culturally and linguistically responsive, that is, whether they "validate, facilitate, liberate, and empower ethnically diverse students" as learners.

REFLECT AND APPLY

What does the Baldwin quote that follows mean to you? How does it connect to your students?

"A child cannot be taught by anyone whose demand, essentially, is that the child repudiate his experience and all that gives him sustenance."

CHAPTER THREE

Practical Application

Culturally and Linguistically Responsive Instructional Strategies That Advance Learning in EL and SEL Populations

"For students who experience disproportionate levels of academic failure, the extent to which the students' language and culture are incorporated into the school program constitutes a significant predictor of academic success." —Jim Cummins (2001)

The cultural and linguistic diversity of the students who traditionally occupy classrooms in the large, urban cities of America has for decades created major challenges for educators. How teachers perceive and respond to cultural diversity and language variation in students greatly impacts whether or not those students will gain access to the core academic curricula, to college preparatory course work, and to career options. Instructional practice is greatly impacted by adverse educator attitude.

Instruction must be culturally relevant and linguistically responsive for EL and SEL students to access rigorous core standards-based curricula. The culturally and linguistically competent educator who must deliver this instruction is one who acknowledges, affirms, and accommodates cultural and linguistic diversity in his or her students, knows how to lower affective filters that block language acquisition and learning, and uses students' prior knowledge, cultural experience, and language as scaffolds to academic language acquisition and learning.

The instructional approaches for ELs and SELs outlined in this chapter are inferred from the premise that the gaps in proficiency levels are wide in part because these students' learning encounters with educators are not fully aligned with their core cultural referents. We believe, as Gay avers "culture counts" (Gay, 2000, p. 8); it matters that culturally and linguistically diverse students bring different ways of speaking, thinking, and interacting to the learning environment, but we also know that because of these differences, their intellectual capabilities are routinely misjudged. SELs in particular are often viewed through deficit lenses and their language, culture, and learning styles are not deemed useful for mediating learning. We accept that cultural and linguistic diversity are strengths and, when acknowledged, affirmed, and integrated into instruction, become useful rubrics for addressing the learning needs of ELLs and SELs.

REFLECT AND APPLY

What does the Nobles quote that follows mean to you?
"Culture is to humans as water is to fish."
Answer individually or in small groups the question: What is water to fish? How does this apply to your students? Reflect on or discuss in small groups the relationship of culture and learning.

Presented in the following pages are five principles of effective teaching and five instructional approaches grounded in CLRP that advance language acquisition and learning in ELs and SELs. They have been affirmed in the research as efficacious for language acquisition and learning in culturally and linguistically diverse students and are put forth here as examples of good teaching methodology for EL and SEL populations.

FIVE PRINCIPLES OF EFFECTIVE TEACHING FOR EL AND SEL STUDENTS

The five culturally responsive principles emphasize important concepts allied with creating learning environments that honor students' home cultures and communities and place the onus on teachers not only to master subject matter but to invest in the hearts and souls of their students, to get to know them, to care about them, and to make positive contributions to their present and future lives. Teachers must know how to accommodate diverse students' learning styles and strengths and be knowledgeable of pedagogy that values diversity, caring, and community and that connects students with each other as well as with the core curricula. These five principles set the stage for instruction mediated through the culture, language, and prior knowledge and experiences that ELs and SELs bring to the learning environment.

PRINCIPLE ONE: KNOW YOUR STUDENTS

All students bring themselves to the learning environment, and getting to know them as members of cultural communities and as learners is prerequisite to good teaching. Often the declaration that teachers must "know your students" is met with retorts like "where do I find the time to study the cultural and linguistic histories of all the different children in my classroom?" The answer to that question is that all the information you need is sitting in front of you in the classroom. The students themselves are the best source for information on who they are culturally, linguistically, and behaviorally and on what their prior knowledge, backgrounds, and interests are. When a student's culture, language, experiences, and interests are acknowledged, validated, and affirmed in the classroom, the door is opened for true learning experiences. Teachers who know their students have a better understanding of their learning styles and strengths, the experiences in which their understandings about the world are positioned, their need profile, and their dreams and aspirations, and it is this knowledge that allows the teacher to teach students in the way they will learn.

Teachers can build relationships with students by gathering and analyzing information about them, their home and community life, their culture and language, their interests and desires, their understandings about the world and how it works, and how they learn. Teachers must schedule time to talk with students, to get to know them as the unique individuals they are, and to affirm that they care about them and about what is going on in their everyday lives. When teachers increase their understanding of who their students are, they increase student engagement and are able to better structure the classroom environment for learning. A simple "I Am" poem completed and shared in the learning community can work wonders in opening the door for student-to-student relationship building as well as between teacher and student. The format for the "I Am" poem is a series of sentence starters to be completed by the student. Fewer stanzas can be used and the sentence starters varied.

First Stanza

> *I am (two special characteristics about you)*
>
> *I wonder*
>
> *I see*
>
> *I want*
>
> *I am (first line of the poem repeated)*

Second Stanza

> *I pretend*
>
> *I feel*
>
> *I worry*
>
> *I cry*
>
> *I am (first line of poem repeated)*

Third Stanza

> *I say*
>
> *I dream*
>
> *I try*

I have used this format successfully with both K–12 and university students.

REFLECT AND APPLY

Construct your own "I Am" poem for use with the students in your classroom.

Consider age, grade, and performance levels in constructing the poem. Also consider cultural communication style preferences in how students are to respond; for example, answers to the prompts may be given orally and/or in writing.

PRINCIPLE TWO: CONNECT INSTRUCTION TO STUDENTS' PRIOR KNOWLEDGE AND EXPERIENCES

The research supports the notion that learners construct concepts from prior knowledge (Gay, 2000; Hurley, Boykin, & Allen, 2005). Prior knowledge represents existing competencies that can be used in the service of attaining new ones. It incorporates what students know and how well they know it and is an important factor that influences both student learning and achievement. As students encounter new knowledge, they must be able to relate it to their existing knowledge framework, allowing them to adjust and expand their understanding of concepts. The everyday knowledge that students bring with them to the classroom is a warehouse of useful ideas for learning, and this prior knowledge, which encompasses different types of knowledge and skills, should be considered in both instructional design and curriculum planning. Hurley, Boykin, and Allen (2005) assert that "learning contexts that include familiar cultural themes are more likely to sustain and enhance students' motivation to engage in required tasks than contexts characterized by unfamiliar themes" (p. 515).

The job of the teacher is to expand preexisting schemas relative to concepts being taught, and for the teacher to do this, he or she must know what the students know—what their existing schemas are. A schema is an abstract concept that represents units of understanding that are joined into relationships with one another. The schemas represent what students already know about a particular concept and are key in making sense of new concepts introduced in the learning environment. Schema Theory suggests that all knowledge is organized into units, and unless linkages are made between the new and the known, learning will not take place. Building on the concept of Schema Theory, it becomes clear that imparting new knowledge requires bridge building. Because learning proceeds primarily from prior knowledge and only secondarily from presented material, when the prior knowledge of diverse learners is at odds with presented material, it may result in students learning something disparate to the teacher's intention. It is important that students bring to the forefront their preexisting understandings of the concepts being taught.

The experiences students bring, their language and existing understandings about the world and their community, are foundational to new learning experiences. Teachers must be well informed about students' prior experiences and understandings to make proper linkages to new knowledge, and students must be consciously aware of their own understandings relative to the new concepts being taught. Both the quantity and quality of students' prior knowledge positively influence knowledge acquisition and the ability to apply higher-order problem-solving skills. It is important for teachers to know what experiences define their students' home and community life because what students already know—their existing competencies—facilitates future learning, the attaining of new competencies.

Teachers can facilitate students' accessing prior knowledge in multiple ways. What follow are two examples of how teachers can build bridges between the known and the unknown, and that will help culturally and linguistically diverse students make the most of new learning experiences.

Prior Knowledge Assessments

Prior knowledge assessments at the beginning of the course and prior to teaching specific concepts can support instruction with EL and SEL students. These valuations can help identify zones of proximal development, useful for establishing starting points of instruction; can bridge gaps in preexisting knowledge; and can facilitate the structuring of cooperative learning groups that support learning in EL and SEL students. A prior knowledge assessment need not be complicated; it can be as simple as asking students to list what they know about the topic or concept about to be discussed. This type of assessment can raise students' prior understandings to consciousness and can provide teachers with a feel for what students already know and what they may have misconstrued. The Cornell Center for Teaching Excellence (2015) suggests asking the following questions when planning your prior knowledge assessment: (1) What do you assume students already know? (2) What kind of questions will help you affirm your assumptions? (3) What are some common misconceptions or myths related to your subject? (4) How are you going to analyze and respond to the data your pre-assessment provides? Some prior assessment strategies suggested by the Cornell Center include the following: a Common Sense Inventory, which requires making a list of 10 to 15 statements related to the course content, including popular misconceptions, and having students mark "true" or "false" next to each statement, or a Background Knowledge Probe, which requires preparing and writing on the board two or three open-ended or multiple-choice questions related to the concept about to be taught that students are asked to respond to in two or three sentences or to circle a response.

Example Background Knowledge Probe: Equator

(1) Have never heard of this.

(2) Have heard of it but don't really know what it is.

(3) Have some idea what this is but not too clear.

(4) Have a clear idea what this is and can explain.

These activities are not to be graded, and students should be informed of this at the beginning of the exercise.

Advance Organizers

Advance organizers are activities completed prior to learning or to introducing new material that help students anticipate, organize, and sometimes reorganize their thinking. They are designed to bridge the gap between what the learner already knows—prior knowledge—and what he or she needs to learn and to orient them to what it is they will be learning. The use of advance organizers has been shown, through research (Ruthkosky & Dwyer, 1996; Mayer, 2003; Joyce, Weil, & Calhoun, 2003), to improve levels of understanding and recall, particularly for culturally and linguistically diverse students. Advance organizers present information that can be used by ELL and SEL students to interpret new, incoming information. They may take different forms including clear teacher instructions, graphic organizers, or what are sometimes referred to as concept maps. The objective is to enhance students' ability to receive, store, and recall information and to provide them with clear orientation to the learning task.

Example: Advance Organizer

Topic/Concept Being Taught	What Do I Know About It?	What Do I Need to Know About It?	What Did I Learn About It?
Mathematical concept: **Fractions**			
Geographical concept: **The North Pole**			

REFLECT AND APPLY

Design an advance organizer that you will use in your classroom when introducing new ideas, concepts, or information to students.

PRINCIPLE THREE: ACTIVELY ENGAGE STUDENTS IN LEARNING

Learning is no longer considered a process of accumulating information; it is the teacher's job to arouse the mind of students and promote self-actualized learning that supports the student in becoming everything he or she is capable of becoming. It is axiomatic that the higher the learner's involvement, the greater potential for learning, a concept supported by the old adage attributed to Confucius: "I hear and I forget. I see and I remember. I do and I understand." Learning is not a passive transfer of knowledge from teacher to student; it is an active process that engages students in a creative act of constructing knowledge, drawing upon their prior knowledge and experience and upon new information. The root or etymological meaning of the word "education" is to "bring out," thus it is not the teacher's job to "pour in" or "fill up" students but to draw out what they already know and use it to mediate new understandings. Linda Darling-Hammond, professor of education at Stanford University, in an address at the National Council on Educating Black Children Conference April 16, 2015, declared, "There is more knowledge in the last ten years, than in the entire history of the world prior to that time." This daunting statistic illuminates the point that teaching cannot be about filling students with facts; teaching must be, as Palmer (2007) avers, about evoking the truth the student holds within.

Teachers of ELL and SEL students must become facilitators of learning, not releasers of information, allowing students to actively learn for themselves. Because active learning places responsibility for learning on the learner, it allows the student to put to use everything they already know and what has just been taught. Active learning engages students in discussion, reflection, and problem solving and encourages critical thinking, analysis, and synthesis of information. For ELL and SEL students being actively engaged in instructional activities that provide opportunities to assemble, arrange, observe, identify, classify, practice, categorize, construct, recall, give examples, organize, decide, describe, and tell, is paramount in instruction.

The purposeful activity of information exchange through reflective dialogue—student-to-student and student-to-teacher talk—that is accountable to the concept(s) being taught and to the learning community, is a powerful tool in active learning and in building community within the classroom. Incorporation of instructional conversations, accountable talk, or Socratic practice strategies encourage mindful engagement with the material being presented. When culturally and linguistically diverse students are actively engaged in the learning and are able to discuss what they are learning, relate it to past experiences, write about it, and apply it to their daily lives, powerful learning takes place. ELs and SELs need student-centered, active learning encounters that enhance comprehension and retention of material presented and propel students to reach their fullest potential as learners.

REFLECT AND APPLY

There is an old adage that says, "The person doing the talking is the one doing the learning."

Conduct an assessment of the amount of teacher talk that transpires during a teaching period. Assess how much instruction time is allocated to student talk around the concepts or ideas being presented. If you are talking more than 25 to 30 percent of the time, begin to reduce your talk time, and encourage more student talk.

PRINCIPLE FOUR: MAKE CLASSROOMS SAFE, CARING LEARNING COMMUNITIES

Caring is viewed as one of the major pillars of CLRP for ethnically diverse students. Caring relationships are characterized by "patience, persistence, facilitation, validation and empowerment for the participants" (Gay, 2000). Students care that you care. Classrooms must be places where students feel respected, valued, and validated, where the learning community is a safety zone in which students are not afraid to speak in whatever language is accessible to them and where they are supported and encouraged in becoming comfortable, competent learners. The classroom as a learning community is a place where genuine relationships are built, where the goal, as Palmer (2007) avers, is not so much helping students to "know" but helping them to "become," to realize their full potential as they make connections between academic learning and living in the real world. The caring teacher, according to Gay (2000), has faith in the ability of all students to learn and is committed to promoting their psycho-emotional well-being as well as their academic success. Valenzuela (1999), in her investigation of academic achievement among immigrant Mexicans and Mexican American students, found a tendency on the part of teachers to objectify culturally and linguistically diverse students and reject a nurturing view of education. This refusal on the part of educators to initiate and nurture genuine caring relationships with diverse students, to affirm them as people who have goals and dreams, hopes and desires, depletes the learning environment of the "mother's milk" of effective instruction, and works against students, not for them.

One of the best ways to promote caring in instruction is through communal and cooperative learning environments. The research supports communal settings as best suited for knowledge building with culturally and linguistically diverse learners, as opposed to individual competitive ones (Hurley et al., 2005; Palmer, 2007). Communal and cooperative learning environments are important culturally responsive teaching strategies for diverse learners because they value difference and provide for supportive learning environments that maximize interaction. There is research that suggests communalism is a "salient cultural theme" exhibited in the socialization experiences of ethnically diverse students (Boykin, Lilja, & Tyler, 2004). The important concepts that define communal learning environments include: (1) social orientation, placing a premium on interactions and relationships with people as opposed to with objects or things; (2) group duty, prioritizing the concerns of the group over personal concerns; (3) identity, making group membership pivotal to one's self-identity; and (4) sharing, accepting that resources are rightfully shared rather than amassed for personal use (Hurley 1999). Similarly, Boykin (1997) examined the influence of learning conditions on African American students' critical thinking, and his findings suggest that "learning in more culturally salient communal environments, may enhance the critical thinking abilities and facilitate the employment of advanced cognitive strategies of low-income African American elementary children" (p. 13). In advocating for a communal relational learning environment in the classroom, Palmer (2007) writes, "Competition is the antithesis of community, an acid that can dissolve the fabric of relationship" (p. 106). He advises that if we are to teach for life change, classrooms must become communities that provide space for feelings, as well as facts, where culturally and linguistically diverse students are inspired to develop genuine, caring relationships; where they learn to care not just about their own achievements but also about the achievements of their classmates; and where cooperative learning is encouraged and mutual respect is fostered.

In cooperative learning settings students with different levels of ability work interdependently in small groups or teams to achieve learning goals. The interaction and opportunities for constructing and negotiating meaning in safe, cooperative learning environments where collaboration, caring, and enhanced communication skills are encouraged are vital for EL and SEL students.

Teachers who care about students, Gay (2000) contends, "honor their humanity, hold them in high esteem, expect high performance from them, and use strategies to fulfil their expectations" (p. 46). Caring teachers engender higher levels of success in their students, and low achievement is not an acceptable option.

REFLECT AND APPLY

Describe what caring in an instructional environment looks like to you, and then list two things you can begin doing to create a more caring learning community and environment in your classroom.

PRINCIPLE FIVE: INCREASE RIGOR AND HOLD HIGH EXPECTATIONS FOR ACADEMIC SUCCESS

Every child has a right to a rigorous, challenging course of study. The belief that some children are not entitled to rigor in instruction has made its way into the belief system of far too many educators and has become the determining factor in selecting dummied-down curricula and restructuring learning environments in ways that do not well serve ELL and SEL students. Linda Darling-Hammond (1997) refers to this "differentiation of curriculum . . . based on presumptions about what students can or should learn" as "education apartheid" (pp. 266–267), and unfortunately it is cultural, linguistic, and low-income ethnic minority students who are most often the targets of this discreditable practice.

What Is Rigor?

Rigor does not mean increasing the workload or the difficulty of assignments; rigor demands thought, engagement, discovery, and targeted effort, and it is measured by the degree to which students gain deeper understandings of ideas and concepts taught. Rigor encourages and motivates students to build their brains through active engagement with learning experiences. A rigorous curriculum is a thinking curriculum that engages students in inquiry, problem solving, reflection, and the active use of knowledge. In a rigorous curriculum concepts are progressively deepened as students raise questions, analyze and synthesize information, interpret texts, and construct solutions.

Rigor is an essential element in learning, and every student regardless of race, color, or creed deserves an instructional curriculum that engages them in high-order thinking and that challenges them to take risks, question, analyze, and synthesize information. No child should be left behind due to restricted opportunities to learn at high levels. President Barack Obama in a speech to the United States Hispanic Chamber of Commerce on March 10, 2009, addressed the urgency of correcting this condition. He said, "It's time to prepare every child, everywhere in America, to out-compete any worker, anywhere in the world. It's time to give all Americans a complete and competitive education from the cradle up through a career. We've accepted failure for far too long."

ELs, SELs, and low-income ethnic minorities must not be relegated to "drill-and-kill," fact-oriented recitation instructional environments. They deserve better, yet the research affirms diverse learners are disproportionally assigned to remedial and low-level classes that afford limited or no access to rigor. ELs and SELs need opportunities to ask high-level questions, reflect, rethink, synthesize, apply, and evaluate new concepts taught, for it is only then that true learning has ensued. Teachers must be open to exploring their personal beliefs and assumptions that lead to low expectations for diverse students and come to understand that ability is not static and all students—given the proper metacognitive tools—can build intelligence. When students have access to a rigorous curriculum, they become mediators of their own learning, actively monitoring, managing, and holding themselves accountable to the learning.

REFLECT AND APPLY

Which of the following aspects of rigor do you promote in your classroom? Begin now to plan how you will infuse them in future instructional activities.

- Active use of knowledge—inquiry, synthesizing information from multiple sources, applying prior knowledge, interpreting texts, formulating hypotheses, and problem solving

(Continued)

(Continued)

- High thinking demand—questioning, challenging assumptions, debating, and reasoning
- Academic conversations—student talk, accountable to what is being discussed, attentive listening, elaboration of ideas, and constructing explanations

CULTURALLY AND LINGUISTICALLY RESPONSIVE INSTRUCTIONAL APPROACHES FOR TEACHERS OF ELs AND SELs

Ensuring equity in accessing rigorous core content curricula for ELs and SELs has proven elusive for too many urban American school districts. ELLs and SELs constitute a large percentage of the students performing below and far below basic in core academic areas. Recent data from national standardized achievement tests indicate that 75 to 80 percent or more of ELL and SEL students are functioning below levels of proficiency in reading, English language arts, and in mathematics at the fourth- and eighth-grade levels. Effectively meeting the language acquisition and learning needs of this traditionally underperforming population will require paradigm shifts away from deficit thinking and concomitant low expectations for language-different students and toward more culturally and linguistically conscious pedagogy.

The research suggests that how teachers perceive their students and define themselves in relation to them determine to a large degree what the educational experiences of students will be. Teachers who have limited knowledge of and who devalue the language, culture, and experiences of students convey messages that negatively impact students' classroom performance and result in lowered aspirations and achievement levels. Listed next are instructional approaches affirmed by the research and shown effective in classrooms in large, urban school districts as efficacious for advancing language acquisition and learning in ELL and SEL populations. Culturally conscious and linguistically responsive teachers will incorporate these instructional approaches into the curriculum to assure equity in accessing core content curricula for culturally and linguistically diverse students.

WHAT CULTURALLY AND
LINGUISTICALLY RESPONSIVE TEACHERS DO

(1) Build their personal knowledge and understanding of the culture, languages, and linguistic histories of ELs and SELs and methods for integrating that knowledge into core instruction.

(2) Infuse the history, culture, experiences, and canons of literature of ELs and SELs into the learning environment and the instructional design.

(3) Use second language acquisition methodologies including contrastive analysis and other strategies that support acquisition of school language and literacy.

(4) Build on the cultural learning styles and strengths of ELs and SELs to support and scaffold access to rigorous core content curricula.

Instructional Approach 1: Build personal knowledge and understanding of the culture, languages, and linguistic histories of ELs and SELs and methods for integrating that knowledge into core instruction.

American educational institutions have produced a paucity of bilingual, bicultural, literate SEL students that may result in part from the failure of educators to use the available knowledge on issues of language variation provided through the linguistic research. Many educators do not understand the languages of SEL students to be different languages but rather see them as indicators of failed attempts to master standard English. There is more than three decades of linguistic research that provide information on the origin and historical development of the language of African American SELs, including its characteristic linguistic features, style, use, and pedagogical implications. There are numerous books and resources on the cultural and linguistic histories of other SEL populations as well. Educators however have not accessed this knowledge or used it in constructing learning environments that would more effectively advance academic language development in SELs. If educators were to take advantage of this knowledge source, it would greatly increase their skill and comfort level for teaching language-different SELs.

Teachers who have limited knowledge of or who devalue the language, culture, and experiences of SELs and ELLs convey messages that negatively impact their classroom performance and that can result in lowered aspirations and achievement levels. Tauber (1997) sustains the assertion that students define themselves through the lens of their teachers, thus affirming the substantial impact teacher attitude has on student performance.

Educators who expect less of students typically demand less, and when teachers have low expectations of students, there is a tendency to engage in behaviors that harvest failure in them. Educating teachers on the cultural and linguistic histories of ELLs and SELs becomes an important strategy for combating negative perceptions about the cognitive, linguistic, and academic abilities of students for whom English and standard English are not native.

Listed next are sample strategies for how teachers in a learning community might acquire the knowledge necessary for structuring or restructuring teaching and learning environments that are culturally and linguistically responsive.

Strategy I

Teachers and administrators implement literature circles at the school site and engage in a review of current literature and research on ELL and SEL populations and on effective methodologies for instructing them. The purpose of professional readings through literature circles is for teachers to develop professional competence for teaching culturally and linguistically diverse student populations by engaging in firsthand knowledge building with original resources and research. Through review and discussion of the literature with colleagues, teachers develop a deeper understanding of the critical concepts, such as CLRP, related to powerful instruction for ELs, SELs, and other underachieving students. The knowledge gleaned from studying the literature is given practical application in the classroom through collaboratively designed lessons, peer coaching, and analysis of student work. Two books excellent for jump-starting this learning experience are *Culturally Responsive Teaching* by Geneva Gay (2002) and *Negotiating Identities* by Jim Cummins (2001).

Strategy II

Support the development of learning communities at the school site that engage teachers as critical friends in lesson study, peer coaching, and analysis of student work as a condition necessary for effectively educating ELs and SELs. Teachers are encouraged to observe each other's instruction, offer feedback in nonthreatening ways, and assist each other in refining instruction through collaborative lesson planning.

Descriptive Activities

- Grade-level student achievement teams (GSATs) at the elementary level and content-specific student achievement teams (CSATs) at the secondary level are learning communities where teachers are engaged in a dynamic process of knowledge building, collaboration, and critical inquiry focused specifically on the implementation of rigorous, content-focused, and culturally and linguistically responsive instruction. The GSATs and CSATs provide a structured atmosphere in which teachers meet and interact meaningfully on a regular basis to review the literature and student assessment data, and to discuss, debate, critique, discover, and construct learning around CLRP. Teachers also engage in collaborative dialogue relative to effective instructional methodologies, lesson planning, student achievement, and optimal instructional resources.

Instructional Approach 2: Infuse the history, culture, and canons of literature of EL and SEL populations into the learning environment and instructional design.

An established truism in education is that for students to be successful academically, they must first be comfortable with themselves. Yet, the research suggests that traditional American school culture reflects the dominant European class and that minority students often become disadvantaged and lose their "perceptions of personal competence" soon after they start their formal schooling (Gay, 2000, Marri, 2005; Ogbu, 2008.) Students who experience difficulty in school often display low self-esteem due to lack of confidence in their potential. If we are to end this trend, teachers must not only cultivate new belief paradigms relative to diverse learners' potential for learning, including raising their expectations relative to achievement, but they must also be able to establish learning communities that affirm EL and SEL students' sociocultural experiences and help them see themselves as capable learners.

ELs and SELs need to see themselves in instruction, and they benefit when their culture is integrated into the school curriculum;

therefore, learning about the cultural background of students and incorporating that knowledge into instruction is a widely recommended intervention (Delpit & Dowdy, 2002; Ladson-Billings, 2005; Ogbu, 2008). If connections are made between the funds of knowledge (practical and intellectual knowledge and skills found among the social networks in students' homes and communities) that students bring to school, teachers can more readily advance new learning. Listed next are sample strategies for making the learning environment more culturally relevant and responsive for ELL and SEL students.

Strategy I

Develop school and classroom environments that acknowledge, accept, affirm, respect, and accommodate cultural diversity.

Descriptive Activities

- Engage students in various activities involving a study of people, cultures, languages, or events by creating dialogue for plays using information in literature and poetry from their own culture and from other cultures.
- Incorporate into instruction cultural art and artifacts, games, pictorial histories, and books on great achievers who validate the importance of the contributions of EL and SEL populations to our world.

  o Have the students pick a cultural artifact from their home to share in class, but first have them interview a person or person who knows about this object. They can construct the questions they will ask, using a KWL graphic organizer (K: What a student already knows, W: What a student wants to know, and L: What a student ultimately learns).

- Have students create a family tree or chart detailing the members of their family and where various members came from and or live. Follow up with a storyboard: How does the family live in America? The storyboard should illustrate four to six scenes of family interactions, and students should write sentences explaining what each scene depicts.
- Expose students to music, literature, and poetry from their own and other cultures.

- o Middle and High School: Introduce students to the concept of a poetry slam. Share videos of this activity, and encourage students to write their own poetry for a classroom poetry slam.

- Involve younger students in storytelling of cultural folktales from around the world, and encourage them to recite poems, rhymes, and songs from their own and other cultures.

  - o Elementary Grades: Have students orally share different jump-rope jingles, then have them in collaborative groups write their own jingles and share with the class.

- Discuss with students the concepts of migration and immigration. Explain that the majority of people who live in America came to this country from other places in the world, spoke different languages, and held different cultural practices. Elaborate on the immigration status of SEL populations as "involuntary" immigrants.

- Invite parents, grandparents, or relatives to be part of the learning community, answer questions, and share information about their personal histories and experiences.

Strategy II

Increase EL and SEL students' knowledge, awareness, and appreciation of their own linguistic histories.

Descriptive Activity

- Teach students about, and provide opportunities for them, to hear spoken the indigenous languages of their ancestors, including West African, Spanish, Hawaiian, and Native Indian languages. These can be obtained from embassies and on the Internet.

- Have students view video clips on language use in America using videos, such as the *Do You Speak American* or *The Story of English*, to begin the discussion of language variation.

- Have students discuss the various cultural groups that live in their community and identify and describe the language and verbal practices observed.

- Have students research biographies of playwrights from their own cultural or linguistic backgrounds and employ a personal narrative in developing a familiar and original script in the voice of their culture that can be produced as a short skit.

- o High School: Introduce works by August Wilson and/or Gary Soto.
- o Read an excerpt from one of the writings (or the whole text over time), and have students analyze the language use.
- o Pull out specific sentences or paragraphs, and have students rewrite them in standard English.
- o Discuss how the essence of the writing changes and what is lost in the translation.
- o Have students in cooperative groups write original scripts in the voice of their culture and share them in class.

- Have students conduct surveys to determine the various languages spoken in the school, community, and classroom, then have them compare and contrast the different languages and cultures in the school and community.
- Have students investigate which language is the most dominant in the community and in the school and hypothesize why a particular language is spoken more than another in those environments.

Strategy III

Infuse the history and culture of ELs and SELs into the instructional design.

Descriptive Activity

- Match print with cultural and community activities (e.g., trips to the mall or the grocery store, playground or gym activities, dance and popular physical movement games, and church and Sunday school experiences).
- Expose students to books and stories about historic and contemporary African American, Mexican American, Native American Indian, and Hawaiian American populations.
- Have students use magazines, books, calendars, travel brochures, and such to create a mural or collage of culturally diverse people and places, then have them generate sentences or paragraphs to describe the people and places they have seen as a result of viewing the pictures or reading the books.
- Involve students in instructional conversations about the universal elements of culture among ancient societies and how

they are evidenced by African Americans, Mexican Americans, and other cultural groups in the United States.

- Using graphic organizers or "thinking maps," have students compare and contrast the language, lifestyles, customs, beliefs, contributions, and family structures of one nation of people to another or to the students' own ethnic groups.
- Integrate primary and secondary cultural sources such as people, documents, photographs, pictures, slides, movies, diaries, ledgers, biographies, or autobiographies into core content instruction.

Instructional Approach 3: Use second language acquisition methodologies including contrastive analysis and other strategies that support acquisition of school language and literacy.

Language represents human experiences and is the medium through which culture conveys its beliefs and values. The research has established that children develop language, oral and written, as they internalize and make sense of the values, routines, and literate actions of the members of their social world (Owocki & Goodman, 2002). Thus second language acquisition instruction for ELs and SELs who are socialized in cultural and linguistic environments that are at variance with the school's culture and language will need to be made relevant and responsive to the cultural literacy experiences they bring to school. Both ELs and SELs need comprehensible input in the target language—academic English—if they are to become proficient speakers, readers, and writers of the language of school and if they are to access the core academic curricula. This comprehensible input is best provided through daily opportunities to see, hear, and interact with more competent users of standard American and academic English (SAE). As EL and SEL students engage with models of the target language (both oral and print), their ability to intuit the structure of SAE is enhanced, and they become more proficient users of the target language forms used in school.

Contrastive analysis and Specially Designed Academic Instruction in English (SDAIE) methodologies are two culturally and linguistically responsive instructional strategies that support second language acquisition and learning in ELs and SELs. These strategies facilitate mastery of SAE oral and written discourse and increase access to core academic content.

SDAIE, which is culturally and linguistically responsive methodology appropriate for teaching core content in English to students for whom English is not native, utilizes instructional strategies that connect with linguistically diverse students' prior knowledge to make core academic concepts comprehensible. SDAIE methodologies, which include graphic organizers, diagrams, and charts that help students organize information and see relationships between concepts—and which incorporate lesson contextualization, low anxiety learning environments, and total physical response—support EL and SEL students in focusing on the essential elements of instruction and in internalizing core concepts as they are taught.

SELs, whose home languages incorporate English vocabulary but differ in structure and grammar from SAE, must come to understand that the language of their home and the language of school differ and that they will need to become proficient in the use of academic English if they are to be successful in American schools and be able to use language appropriately in cross-cultural situations. To facilitate language and literacy acquisition in SELs, teachers need to understand the process of first language acquisition, the general principals of how languages are structured, as well as the process of second language acquisition. They also need to be knowledgeable of the characteristic linguistic features of SEL languages and how they differ from SAE and must then know how to infuse this knowledge into the instructional curriculum. When SELs understand the origin of their home language and how it differs structurally from the language of school, the language of school becomes more comprehensible, and their ability to use the target language—academic English—improves.

Contrastive analysis—the systemic study of the distinctive elements in two different languages with an objective of identifying their structural differences and similarities—has been shown to be an effective, linguistically responsive methodology for facilitating mastery of SAE in SEL populations (Taylor, 1991). It is a strategy that provides SEL and upper-level EL students opportunities to hear, compare and contrast, and practice patterns of SAE. Taylor looked at infusing linguistic knowledge into instruction through the use of contrastive analysis to support standard English language and literacy development in African American SELs. Teachers were trained in the use of contrastive analysis techniques—comparing and contrasting the linguistic structure of the home language and the target language to be acquired—and after employing these strategies over an 11-month period, their students showed a 59 percent reduction in the use of "nonstandard" language features in their written work, whereas the teachers in the study who used traditional language arts approaches saw no decrease in the use of "nonstandard" features in their students' writing but instead saw a slight increase (8.5 percent) in the use of these features.

As SELs become more familiar with the grammatical structures of the language of school as contrasted with the structure of their home language, they increase their metalinguistic and metacognitive awareness and are better able to self-edit their oral and written language for dissimilarities in grammar, vocabulary, and syntax and to use SAE proficiently in appropriate contexts.

Strategy I

Incorporate SDAIE methodology in instruction throughout the instructional day.

Descriptive Activities

- Integrate the use of graphic organizers into oral and written language exercises.
- Demonstrate and model oral and verbal behaviors in academic English expected to be mastered by EL and SEL students, for example, questioning, high-order thinking, analyzing and synthesizing information, summarizing, restating, and so on.
- Tap prior knowledge of EL and SEL students to make schematic linkages to new learning. Teachers must become familiar with the background knowledge that EL and SEL students bring to the learning environment and how to use that knowledge as a rubric for learning.
- Integrate listening, speaking, reading, and writing across the curriculum.
- Emphasize the development of higher-order thinking skills with EL and SEL students moving from simple to complex thinking.

Strategy II

Incorporate contrastive analysis strategies into daily English language arts instruction.

Descriptive Activities

Use these contrastive analysis techniques:

- Linguistic Contrastive Analysis
  - o Use literature, poetry, songs, plays, student-elicited sentences, or prepared story scripts that incorporate examples of specific contrasts between SAE grammar and the grammatical structures that characterize the different languages of SELs.

- **Sample second-grade contrastive analysis activity:**
  - o Have students read the book *Flossie and the Fox* by Patricia McKissack.
  - o Ask students to find their favorite thing Flossie said and their favorite thing the fox said. Write the sentences out.
  - o Have students compare and contrast the language the fox uses and the language Flossie uses. Discuss school and home languages.
  - o Have students rewrite Flossie's sentence in standard English.

- Contextual Contrastive Analysis
  - o The student reads or is told a story that is heavily embedded with the target form (SAE) and is then required to retell the story. The student's story retelling is taped and compared and contrasted with the language of the text.

- Situational Contrastive Analysis
  - o Students contrast and analyze the mainstream and non-mainstream versions of targeted language forms with an emphasis on situational appropriateness, that is, communication, environment, audience, purpose, and function.

- Elicited Contrastive Analysis
  - o The teacher elicits spontaneous verbalizations or responses from students about material read or presented and uses these in-class teachable moments for comparing and contrasting the home and school language.

Source: Adapted with permission from the work of Lorraine Cole (1991).

The Benefits of Contrastive Analysis for ELs and SELs

- Increased ability to recognize the grammatical differences between the language of school and the language of home

- Enhanced ability to edit their own work for SAE structure including differences in grammar, vocabulary, and syntax
- Greater facility in the use of standard English structure in its oral and written forms
- Enhanced appreciation and acceptance of the home language and the language of school

Strategy III

Provide consistent models of SAE throughout the instructional day.

Descriptive Activities

- Incorporate the use of free voluntary reading (FVR) and silent sustained reading (SSR) of mainstream literature to engage EL and SEL students with models of SAE.
- Integrate listening centers and audio books into daily instruction to allow ELs and SELs to hear SAE in its spoken form.
- Read aloud to students from mainstream literature on a daily basis.
- Model and encourage conversations, questioning, and "talk" in the learning environment.
- Provide opportunities for students to speak for a variety of audiences and purposes, including opportunities for storytelling and story retelling.
- Provide opportunities for role-playing, recited speeches, debates, and script reading.

Strategy IV

Build academic language and vocabulary through the development of a personal thesaurus of conceptually coded words.

Descriptive Activity

Emphasize vocabulary development around authentic events, prior knowledge, and students' lives. Each EL and SEL student should own a personal thesaurus developed in the context of the classroom. Teachers use students' prior knowledge and vocabulary to make schematic linkages to, and increase understanding of, academic vocabulary that students are then encouraged to incorporate into daily writing

			H
Hatin'	**Hating**	**Hungry**	**Student's Own Words**
jealous envious invidious	abhorring detesting loathing	famished ravenous _____	Synonyms from Thesaurus (Academic Vocabulary)
"lovin' on"	esteeming		Antonyms

assignments. The thesaurus consists of 26 pages, one page for each letter in the alphabet, and is formatted as seen here.

Words from the students' known vocabulary are placed in the top box and the teacher provides, or students look up in a thesaurus, academic synonyms that are then written on the lines below. EL and SEL students are encouraged to use their personal thesaurus in writing activities, incorporating the words on the lines—the academic vocabulary—in their daily writing experience. The bottom box is for antonyms.

Instructional Approach 4: Build on the cultural learning styles and strengths of ELs and SELs to support and scaffold access to rigorous core content curricula.

Culture is central to shaping the educational process. The way people communicate, think, learn, and interact with others is a direct result of their home and community cultural experiences. People from different cultures think differently and learn differently and thus have different cultural learning styles. Teachers who instruct ELs and SLs must become familiar with the cognitive, communication, and interaction styles and strengths these students bring to the classroom. Keefe (1979) defines "learning style" as "characteristic cognitive, affective, and physiological behaviors that serve as relatively stable indicators of how learners perceive, interact, and respond to the learning environment" (p. 4). The principle assumption in learning style theory is that students with similar intellectual potential will, as a result of how they are socialized culturally, display their cognitive abilities differently (Ladson-Billings, 2009; O'Neil, 1990; Villegas & Lucas, 2002).

Many researchers feel that accommodating students' distinct learning, cognitive, and communication styles in instruction can make a difference in their learning (Boykin, 2001; Delpit & Dowdy, 2002; Ladson-Billings, 2009). As educators we have an obligation to teach students in the ways that they learn.

Learning styles vary with cultural and ethnic identity. The learning style research reports, for example, that African Americans as a group have distinct ways of processing information, interacting, communicating, and learning. Hilliard (1992) for example, asserts that the high degree of "within-group socialization" that exists among African Americans, in general, stems from a long and continuing history of racial segregation and economic discrimination. In his study conducted in California, Hilliard contrasted African and African American culture with European and European American culture. He concluded that a unique African American core culture could be empirically described and that cultural behavioral style distinctions exist. He further extrapolated that traditional American schools are "encapsulated in a style that mimics the cultural style of most European Americans" (p. 373) and is therefore not a good fit for African American SELs. Hilliard deduced that African Americans view their environment as a whole rather than in isolated parts; prefer intuitive rather than deductive or inductive reasoning; approximate concepts of space, number, and time; attend to people stimuli rather than object stimuli; and rely on nonverbal as well as verbal communication. Boykin's (1997) research findings revealed that African American children's highest performance in comprehension and recall emerges when high-movement expressive content is presented in a high-movement expressive context. European American children in his studies, on the other hand, scored highest when low-movement expressive content was presented in a low-movement expressive context.

A student's culture is a reflection of his or her life as it is experienced and understood, and teachers who instruct ELs and SELs must accommodate the distinct cultural, learning, and communication styles they bring to the instructional environment. They must develop culturally consistent ways of interacting with students from cultures different from their own and learn to adjust instruction so that learners from diverse cultures are affirmed in instruction and their cultural referents are accommodated.

Teachers of diverse learners will need to critically examine themselves and their methods of instruction relative to their responsiveness to diversity in students. Much of traditional instructional pedagogy in American schools, because it is grounded in Eurocentric ideologies, privileges the dominant culture and neglects non-Eurocentric students. Cummins (2001) asserts that "minority students can become empowered *only* [italics added] through interactions with educators who have critically examined and, where necessary, challenged the educational (and social) structure within which they operate" (p. 6). Culturally responsive teachers, Irvin and Armento (2001) contend, view the differences diverse students such as ELs and SELs bring to the classroom as strengths rather than deficits and act to accommodate these differences to remove barriers to learning and enhance academic achievement. Culturally competent teachers acknowledge and incorporate diverse learners' funds of knowledge—the practical and intellectual knowledge and skills students gain from their family and cultural backgrounds—into the curriculum to make classrooms more inclusive. Teachers who have a good understanding of cultural learning style differences are better positioned to support ELs and SELs in the transition to becoming bilingual and bicultural.

Strategy I

Create communal and cooperative learning environments that promote collective responsibility for learning in students and build on the cultural experiences of EL and SEL students.

Descriptive Activity

- Group students' desks to encourage social interaction and collaborative learning. Create a communal learning environment for instruction.
- Incorporate instructional conversations as part of daily academic discourse.
- Encourage students to support each other in learning; remove competition from the environment.
- Utilize cooperative learning groups routinely for instructional activities, for example, Think-Pair-Share.

CHAPTER FOUR

Fostering Literacy With CLRP

L iteracy is an extension of natural language learning, and when students are not part of the mainstream culture, speak a different language, or bring literacy experiences to the classroom that do not match school literacy experiences, instruction will need to be modified to assure that learning occurs. The literacy acquisition classroom for ELs and SELs must be a holistic natural language environment filled with authentic language experiences and literacy activities that include being read to, collaborative listening, exposure to books that relate to their experiences, and free voluntary reading and where students can begin to see themselves as readers and writers.

Our preferred definition of literacy interprets it as a social practice, as an act people perform with various texts to engage in meaning making in social communities. This definition draws on Vygotsky's sociocultural theory of human learning and his social constructivist views about literacy, which suggests that literacy acquisition is a complex interactive and interpretative process and social factors are key determinants in its development. Vygotsky, in his seminal work, *Mind in Society: The Development of Higher Psychological Processes*, emphasizes social interaction as key in transforming cultural literacy practices into higher intellectual functions. He believes literacy acquisition involves much more than the accumulation of simple skills or isolated skill activities; rather, he contends the sociocultural context surrounding the learning is of great significance. His perspective affirms that all children regardless of cultural or linguistic background can achieve high levels of literacy provided their teachers adjust instruction in culturally and linguistically responsive ways (Vygotsky, 1978).

American educational institutions place great emphasis on print or book literacy, but contrary to popular belief, there is no single literacy, instead there are a variety of literacy practices found within varying cultural contexts in students' everyday lives (Street, 1995). It is these cultural literacy practices diverse students bring to the classroom that must be acknowledged and accommodated in instruction.

The Institute for Learning (n.d.) at the University of Pittsburgh suggests that in the ideal learning environment students are apprenticed in subject areas as they avail themselves to "masters" in science, history, mathematics, and literature. They contend that it is through these "intellective relationships" with humans and text that students learn to think, speak, analyze, interpret, and write as scientists, historians, mathematicians, and authors. Fundamental and perhaps prerequisite to students' ability to function effectively as apprentices in school learning environments is the possession of basic literacy skills, that is, the ability to speak, read, and write in the language of instruction. Thus, if teachers are to fully engage EL and SEL students in meaningful ways with content knowledge, the acquisition of these basic skills is requisite. If ELs and SELs are to access rigorous core curricula, they must become literate in the forms of English that appear in textbooks, on standardized tests, in newspapers, in magazines, and in consumer contracts. Without these basic skills the ability to effectively negotiate learning environments, construct meaning, and apprentice as scientists, historians, and mathematicians becomes unrealizable.

Students who are learning to read in a second language, ELLs and SELs, experience more problems than students whose home language matches the language of school (LeMoine 2001). Some of the problems result from a lack of familiarity with the semantic and grammatical constraints of school language, but problems can also result from teachers' devaluation and rejection of the students' home language. EL and SEL students need opportunities to engage in and see school literacy practices demonstrated, but they must also be provided opportunities to validate and build upon the rich language and literacy experiences they bring from home. A classroom for ELs and SELs that is conducive to literacy acquisition must be a community where students are comfortable using their home language and taking risks as they master academic language and acquire literacy skills. An environment of this type will provide ELs and SELs with opportunities to learn to value reading and writing as instruments for investigating and enlarging their world.

DEVELOPMENT OF EMERGENT LITERACY SKILLS

Early language experiences are culturally determined and serve as important precursors to literacy. One such experience is being read to. The research confirms that children who are read to prior to school develop phonemic awareness—the ability to hear sounds within a word when it is spoken—which is an important first step in learning to read (Krashen, 2004). Rhyming, singing, and reading out loud to children help develop this skill, and it is an important precursor to phonics instruction. However, it is important to note that being read to prior to school may not be part of the early literacy experiences of some ELs or of most SELs. Storytelling, for example, more likely characterizes the early literacy experiences of African American, Native American, Mexican American, and Hawaiian American SEL populations, and whereas it is a rich literacy experience that fosters phonemic awareness, it does not nurture associations of sounds and words to print. Thus when EL and SEL students arrive at school in kindergarten, school must become the venue for being read to and for the provision of other pre-literacy language experiences they have not been exposed to in the context of their culture. A balanced instructional approach to literacy acquisition that incorporates both meaning construction (language experience) and explicit phonics is culturally and linguistically appropriate and will work best for ELs and SELs who bring language and literacy experiences to the classroom that differ from European-centered traditions.

MEANING CONSTRUCTION AND LANGUAGE EXPERIENCE

Readers read and writers write to gain or convey meaning, thus a meaning construction approach to reading, balanced with phonics tied to the context of the language the child uses, is a good match for language-different populations. Pressley and Allington (2014) contend a balanced literacy approach—which engages students in the full process of reading and writing—perhaps best explains the substantial success of exemplary first-grade teachers in teaching all children to read. It is imperative that literacy acquisition for EL and SEL students take place in learning environments that welcome language and cultural variation and that draw upon students' language experiences and prior knowledge to mediate learning (Cummins, 2000; Krashen, 2004).

The language experience approach to literacy development, which fosters the development of reading and writing through the use of personal experiences and oral language, is culturally and linguistically responsive and therefore ideal for ELs and SELs. This approach to literacy acquisition creates a natural bridge between the spoken word and the written word and between the learner and print. Language experience accommodates home literacy experiences and integrates all of the communication skills, listening, speaking, reading, and writing into learning. This approach to literacy builds upon the students' language and prior knowledge, and as students engage in shared literacy experiences and see their own experiences recorded in writing, they are better able to understand the literacy process. For EL and SEL students whose early literacy experiences did not include being read to, this culturally and linguistically responsive mediated language experience will help them make the connection between what is said (words) and what is written (print) and teach them to value their own literacy experiences, communities, and cultures.

PHONICS

The phonetic method of teaching reading places emphasis on auditory analysis of agreement between oral and written language and requires that learners be able to isolate and identify the distinct phonemes of their language and relate them to graphic signs. Because EL and SEL students learn best when engaged in experiences that build on what they know, they will benefit most from teaching of phonics skills in context, when it is combined with meaningful reading and writing in language experience activities, or with meaningful reading and writing of whole texts. This contextual phonics provides opportunities to acquire phonemic analysis, alphabetic, and phonic skills in the context of both the home language and the language of school.

CULTURALLY RELEVANT
LITERATURE IN THE CLASSROOM

We know from the research that young children who are read to before formal schooling have a good understanding of the relationships between oral and written language (McQuillan & Krashen, 2008). With EL and SEL students, because being read to may not have been part of their early literacy experiences, the classroom has to become the venue for building a relationship between oral language and print and for intuiting concepts about print that are foundational to developing reading and spelling strategies. Opportunities to link storytelling to literacy, as in language experience activities, and to be read to must be part of daily instruction for ELs and SELs. A classroom library and comfortable reading environments are important for creating a community of readers in the classroom that encourages free voluntary reading. When EL and SEL students are provided opportunities to engage with literature that reflects their own culture, language and experiences—culturally relevant literature—they are more motivated to read, and their cultural identity is affirmed Harris (1995). Introducing into the classroom oral literature in the form of cultural folktales and storytelling will help establish important linkages between the home language and literacy experiences of ELs and SELs.

ELs and SELs as second language readers will need support in the development of academic vocabulary, syntactic development, and cultural knowledge. Their limited familiarity with standard English syntax may impair their ability to identify important syntactic relationships in standard American English, and their limited standard English vocabulary may cause difficulty using semantic cues for making predictions and comprehending what they read. Second language acquisition methodologies have been shown to be effective in facilitating mastery of standard American English in both ELs and SELs, specifically, acquisition of standard English grammar, syntax, and vocabulary (Cummins, 2000). Early learning experiences, which involve understanding messages and making sense out of print, form the basis for learning to read and write, similarly to how understanding verbal messages aid in acquiring spoken language. Reading requires readers to draw upon their personal knowledge about the topic, thus school literacy experiences must incorporate the language and cultural literacy experiences the child brings to school.

For ELs and SELs the classroom must become the venue for building relationships between oral language and print and for developing emergent literacy skills. Increased reading results in improved literacy development. Students who read more perform better on tests of reading comprehension, vocabulary, writing, and grammar (Krashen, 2004). Harris (1995) reports that the benefits derived from increased reading include improved comprehension, increased vocabulary levels, enhanced critical-thinking skills, enjoyment of the creative uses of language and art, and exposure to a variety of linguistic models. Literacy acquisition for ELs and SELs must build on the home language and literacy patterns, experiences, and funds of knowledge these students bring with them to the classroom. Listed next are some sample strategies that promote literacy acquisition in ELL and SEL students.

Strategy I

Use multiple reading strategies and approaches (e.g., learning experience or whole language and contextual phonics) to enhance students' ability to read with accuracy, fluency, and comprehension.

Descriptive Activities

- Provide opportunities for independent reading during class time.
- Provide opportunities for students to speak for a variety of audiences and purposes, including opportunities for storytelling and story retelling.

Incorporate contextual phonics as a part of literacy instruction.

Descriptive Activities

- Teach phonics in context with meaningful reading and writing.
- Address homophones created in the context of the home language—for example, in the African American language: cold–coal, fine–find, and so on.
- Provide opportunities for consistent exposure to the oral and written discourse patterns of standard English.
- Emphasize word-final sound clusters first in phonics instruction with SELs.

Strategy II

Match print with oral language experiences by incorporating language experience activities into instruction.

Descriptive Activities

- Read to students daily from books that reflect their experiences, and openly discuss content to help students make linkages between the spoken word and print.
- Integrate listening centers that include culture-specific folklore, storytelling, audio books, and literature that provides opportunities for students to hear the language of school modeled. Have students record their own stories, transcribe them in writing, and analyze them for appropriate use of "school language."
- Build a classroom library that includes culturally relevant literature, magazines, and community newspapers that reflect students' community, home life, personal interests, cultural background, and language. Include technology—books on tape, computers, CD players, headphones, LCD projectors, TV/VCR, video cameras, and electronic thesauruses—that can be used in the classroom to facilitate language and literacy acquisition.
- Provide opportunities for students to write every day. Use journals, writing portfolios, and other resources.

Strategy III

Conduct contrastive analysis activities daily to support phonetic analysis and second language acquisition.

Descriptive Activities

- Provide opportunities for students to compare and contrast poetry, songs, and stories written in the home languages of SELs and in standard American English.
- Use literature and samples of students' daily oral and written language to engage in contrastive analysis and to support the acquisition of standard American English.

- Use the editing phase of the writing process as a vehicle for analyzing and identifying standard English structure.
- Make literature written in the voice of students' culture available to them in the classroom for enjoyment and for contrastive analysis use.

Strategy IV

Create a classroom environment that facilitates school language and literacy acquisition in ELs and SELs.

- Create a print-rich environment that includes writing centers, teacher- and student-generated lists, word walls, message boards, songs, chants, big books, and journals.
- Group students' desks to encourage social interaction and cooperative and collaborative learning.
- Integrate listening, speaking, reading, and writing into the daily curriculum through readers' theater and dramatic performances.
- Engage students in instructional conversations accountable to the learning.

Strategy V

Build academic vocabulary by expanding the students' personal thesaurus of conceptually coded words.

Descriptive Activities

- Encourage each student to develop a personal thesaurus of conceptually coded words that is built on prior knowledge and vocabulary.
- Encourage vocabulary development in the context of communicating ideas.
- Focus on vocabulary development with an emphasis on synonyms, antonyms, prefixes, and suffixes.
- Motivate students to appreciate literature and the role it plays in developing personal vocabularies.
- Emphasize vocabulary development around authentic events and student lives balanced with dictionary use.

A basic premise of this text is that language is fundamental to learning and that mastery of academic language is critical for accessing core content curricula. It is an important gatekeeper, and students who are not proficient speakers, readers, and writers of this language will not do well in American educational institutions. As educators we are committed to assuring excellence in education for all students and to guaranteeing that ELs and SELs will reach their fullest potential and become the leaders in society that they are destined to be.

REFLECT AND APPLY

Select a culturally relevant, grade-level appropriate literature title, and read it to your students.

If you teach middle or high school, plan to read the first 10 to 15 minutes of the class until the book is completed. Take note of how your students respond to this activity.

CHAPTER FIVE

Assessing for Culturally and Linguistically Responsive Indicators

This chapter provides teachers with tools for assessing the degree to which instruction is culturally and linguistically responsive. An assortment of checklists and rubrics, adapted from tools developed for use in the Los Angeles Unified School District's Academic English Mastery Program, a program developed by Noma LeMoine, and for which she served as director from its inception in 1989 until 2009, is provided to assist educators with assessing the degree to which their instruction is culturally and linguistically responsive.

The first tool is a self-assessment for teachers to facilitate reflection on whether or not their classrooms are culturally compatible; next is a checklist for assessing whether or not instruction is culturally and linguistically responsive to students. The next tool provides a list of key culturally and linguistically responsive instructional methodologies that support language acquisition and learning in ELL and SEL populations, and the last tool is an observation and support tool for mainstream English language development (MELD) instruction for SELs. This final support tool delineates important components of MELD instruction defined as the development of speaking, reading, and writing in SAE, to be effectively implemented in the classroom.

Is Your Classroom Culturally Compatible?

This quick self-assessment tool is designed to increase teachers' awareness of their own teaching and learning environment relative to its relevance and responsiveness to cultural diversity. Teachers are encouraged to respond to and reflect on each question and reassess themselves until success is achieved.

Teacher Self-Assessment

This self-assessment tool allows teachers to rate their teaching and classroom environment to determine where they are in implementing a culturally compatible classroom. The scale ranges from 1 to 5 with 5 representing *being culturally responsive*, 3 meaning *just beginning to put into practice*, and 1 referring to *still seeking understanding and resources.*

Score: 45–50 = Culturally Competent Classroom **45 or less** = Needs Work

Are cultural images and artifacts representative of your student population displayed?

1   2   3   4   5

Do you have learning centers that capitalize and focus on the different learning modalities and intelligences present in your students?

1   2   3   4   5

Do you encourage interpersonal interactions and a sense of family and community?

1   2   3   4   5

Do you allow students to help each other and to work together on a frequent basis?

1   2   3   4   5

Do you find ways to engage all students in each lesson?

1   2   3   4   5

When giving an assignment, do you provide a global view of the task as well as a step-by-step plan for what groups and individuals are to accomplish?

1   2   3   4   5

Do you model and schedule opportunities to practice the ideas and concepts before you require students to demonstrate or test their understanding?

1   2   3   4   5

Do you operate in the classroom as a guide and facilitator rather than a performer in front of an audience?

1   2   3   4   5

Does engagement mean more to you than asking and responding to questions or worksheets?

1   2   3   4   5

Do you use the arts (fine art, music, and literature) and multimedia as alternative ways in which students can gain knowledge of concepts and ideas?

1   2   3   4   5

CLRI Checklist

The CLRI checklist is designed to support teachers, principals, and support staff in becoming familiar with quality indicators of CLRP. It identifies critical teacher actions and corresponding student behaviors that signal the teaching and learning environment is responsive to diversity in positive and productive ways. The tool can be used by teachers as a self-assessment and by administration as an evaluative tool.

CHECKLIST FOR CULTURALLY AND LINGUISTICALLY RESPONSIVE INSTRUCTION

This guide provides teachers and administrators with a quick look at teacher and student CLRI quality indicators and their alignment with student outcomes.

☐ The teacher creates an accepting, affirmative, risk-free classroom environment in which the culture and language of each student is validated, valued, and respected and authentic accomplishments are regularly recognized.	☐ The students are relaxed, comfortable, confident learners, eager to learn and willing to take risks and put forth and sustain high levels of effort.
☐ The teacher incorporates CLRP into rigorous core instruction (uses the cultural knowledge, prior experiences, frames of reference, and performance styles of students to make learning encounters relevant and effective).	☐ The students are responding to instruction in productive comfort zones and demonstrating sustained effort in meeting high standards.
☐ The teacher demonstrates knowledge and understanding of issues of language variation in SELs and ELs and incorporates appropriate strategies to support academic English mastery.	☐ The students are engaged in activities that show understanding and awareness of the linguistic structures of academic language and use them proficiently in speaking, reading, and writing.
☐ The teacher infuses culturally relevant literature and instructional materials into academically rigorous curricula organized around concepts that students are expected to know deeply.	☐ The students engage in active reasoning about important concepts supported by a wide selection of culturally relevant instructional materials and resources.
☐ The teacher employs strategies throughout the curriculum, including contrastive analysis, a personal thesaurus, and accountable talk, that facilitate the students' mastery of academic English and use of language that sustains learning.	☐ The students are actively engaged in activities that facilitate mastery of SAE, including classroom talk that is accountable to the learning community and to rigorous thinking.

☐ The teacher promotes increased confidence, problem-solving behaviors, and the development in students of habits of mind that empower them to achieve their full potential.	☐ The classroom is a student-centered community so that the students have opportunities to interact, problem solve, question, collaborate, explore, reflect, and make decisions.
☐ The teacher demonstrates knowledge of the learning styles and strengths of culturally diverse students and builds upon students' learning strengths to develop self-monitoring and self-management skills that promote academic growth.	☐ The students are visibly engaged in rigorous activities that tap into their personal learning styles and are making use of higher-order thinking and metacognitive skills to manage their own learning.
☐ The classroom environment is culturally relevant and responsive to the students and sets clear expectations by defining what students are expected to learn and displaying criteria and models of work that meets standards.	☐ The students make positive connections to high achievers in their culture, set goals for their own effort, and learn to see themselves as scholars.

KEY CULTURALLY AND LINGUISTICALLY RESPONSIVE INSTRUCTIONAL STRATEGIES THAT SUPPORT ELs AND SELs

This grid delineates six key culturally and linguistically responsive instructional strategies that are efficacious for advancing language acquisition and learning in ELs and SELs. It includes student responses to instruction that teachers should observe as outcomes when instruction is culturally and linguistically responsive. The strategies delineated are (1) contrastive analysis, (2) making cultural connections, (3) use of advance graphic organizers, (4) communal and cooperative learning environments in the classroom, (5) academic language development (ALD), and (6) instructional conversations accountable to the learning.

Key Culturally and Linguistically Responsive Instructional Methodologies That Support ELs and SELs	
INSTRUCTIONAL STRATEGY	**CLASSROOM OBSERVABLES**
Contrastive Analysis: *The systematic study of a pair of languages with a view to identifying their structural differences and similarities. This strategy promotes the acquisition of academic language in SELs and upper-level ELs and helps them become proficient readers, writers, and speakers of SAE.*	**SUPPORTING ACQUISITION OF SAE** ✓ Demonstrates knowledge and awareness of the structure of nonstandard languages ✓ Uses literature and samples of students' oral and written language to engage in contrastive analysis ✓ Uses the revision phase of the writing process to edit written work for standard English structure ✓ Provides opportunities for students to compare and contrast poetry and songs written in standard and nonstandard languages ✓ Uses students' work samples to demonstrate an understanding and awareness of the linguistic structures of SAE ✓ Demonstrates ability to articulate an understanding of the linguistic requirements of varying communication situations and use language appropriate to different contexts
Making Cultural Connections: • Activating prior knowledge • Connecting instruction to students' lives to increase motivation, engagement, and learning • Infusing the history and culture of students into core instruction • Understanding and utilizing students' cultural frames of reference • Utilizing culturally relevant literature • Creating authentic learning experiences	**CONSTRUCTING A CULTURALLY AFFIRMING CONTEXT FOR LEARNING** ✓ Maintains a classroom library that contains culturally conscious literature, magazines, and newspapers reflective of students' home life, interests, cultural background, and language ✓ Provides opportunities for students to make critical connections and give application to meaningful, real-world issues by activating background knowledge ✓ Assesses learning experiences for progress toward meeting core content standards ✓ Utilizes culturally relevant literature and materials in listening centers and MELD ✓ Validates real-life experiences with instructional activities ✓ Has students participate daily in authentic learning experiences giving application to the content ✓ Incorporates music, movement, and hands-on activities into daily instruction

Advance Graphic Organizers:	**ORGANIZING CONCEPTS TO FACILITATE LEARNING**
Visual tools and representations of information provide students with clear orientation to the learning task and show the relationships among ideas and that support critical thinking. Their effective use promotes active learning that helps students construct knowledge, organize thinking, and visualize abstract concepts.	✓ Demonstrates enhanced ability to receive, store, and recall information ✓ Models use of a variety of graphic organizers to ready students for learning and build concept relationships ✓ Engages students in activities to construct knowledge and synthesize important information
Communal and Cooperative Learning Environments:	**CREATING A COLLABORATIVE AND AFFIRMING LEARNING ENVIRONMENT**
Supportive and motivating environments promote learning and caring. Working cooperatively and collaboratively in small groups to achieve an instructional goal, students learn faster and more efficiently, increase time on task, have greater retention, and feel more positive about the learning experience.	✓ Introduces the concept of the classroom as a family structure and builds on this concept in ways that affirm high achievement and academic success as an objective for all students ✓ Encourages students routinely to support each other in learning activities ✓ Provides opportunities for students to interact cooperatively with their peers to brainstorm, explain, question, disagree, persuade, and problem solve ✓ Provides opportunities for students to demonstrate their understanding of academic concepts in varied formats that reflect their preferred learning styles and strengths ✓ Integrates group learning tasks, discussions, and presentations into daily instruction ✓ Emphasizes small-group activities to encourage language development and sharing of ideas ✓ Allows SELs and ELs to maximize the amount of time available for hearing and using language in low-risk cooperative learning environments ✓ Arranges classroom seating to reflect regular collaborative learning opportunities ✓ Cocreates classroom norms and other procedures with students

(Continued)

(Continued)

Academic Language Development (ALD):	SUPPORTING ORAL AND WRITTEN LANGUAGE DEVELOPMENT
Teach academic vocabulary by connecting it to the conceptual knowledge and vocabulary that students acquire in the context of their home and community environments. ALD affirms prior knowledge and promotes increased ability in students to communicate their ideas orally and in writing using academic English.	✓ Utilizes a personal thesaurus to support students' oral and written development of academic vocabulary in the context of communicating ideas ✓ Focuses on vocabulary development with an emphasis on synonyms, antonyms, and suffixes ✓ Engages students in the writing process on a daily basis utilizing journals for ungraded writing activities (pre-writes, quick writes, response writing, etc.) ✓ Utilizes listening centers that model school language using culturally relevant books on tape ✓ Results in student work that reflects appropriate use of academic vocabulary and demonstrates progressive contextual understanding of concepts through oral presentations
Instructional Conversations: These discussions are accountable to the learning community and help students arrive at a deeper understanding of new ideas and concepts. They develop critical thinking and language skills by making connections between academic content and students' prior knowledge, and cultural experiences.	SUPPORTING STUDENT-CENTERED HIGHER-ORDER THINKING AND SPEAKING ✓ Weaves together students' prior knowledge with pertinent background information on new material to build deeper understanding of text. ✓ Engages students in classroom discussions with each other and with the teacher to advance deeper understandings of core academic concepts ✓ Elicits student input while integrating academic content in discussions to promote deeper student inquiry in relation to instructional areas of focus. ✓ Promotes use of text, pictures, and reasoning to support an argument or position ✓ Integrate oral language development into all curricular areas ✓ Co-constructs knowledge with students through interactive discussion, connected turns, and comments that build upon previous ones ✓ Acts as a collaborator and encourages students to volunteer or otherwise influence the selection of speaking turns as they work to construct meaning from text

STRATEGIC OBSERVATION AND SUPPORT TOOL

This observation tool is designed to assist schools with the implementation of an MELD program for SELs. SELs are entitled to and should receive systemic support in acquiring proficiency in the language of school. A designated time allocation of 30 to 45 minutes per day for second language acquisition instruction is recommended. An MELD center, which should be a part of all classrooms that have SEL students, includes an audio center with books on tape; various contrastive analysis activities that address phonology, grammar, and syntax of SAE; books for free voluntary reading; and a writing center. This support tool can be used by teachers for self-assessment and by administration at the school for evaluative purposes.

INSTRUCTIONAL OBSERVATION AND SUPPORT TOOL

MELD Instruction for SELs

MELD refers to the development of speaking, reading, and writing skills in SAE. It is designed to address the specific language acquisition and learning needs of SELs. This support tool delineates components important for MELD instruction to be effectively implemented.

SCHOOL: _____ Grade Level/Course: _____

TEACHER'S NAME: _____ DATE: _____

Circle one of following:

(1 = no evidence; 2 = little evidence; 3 = adequate evidence; 4 = strong evidence)

MELD period is reflected on the posted classroom schedule.

1   2   3   4

SEL students receive 30 to 45 minutes of MELD instruction daily.

YES   NO

MELD instruction is integrated, as appropriate, into the independent workshop time (IWT) of the core literacy program.

1   2   3   4

The MELD center is visible and well stocked with appropriate materials to support student language and literacy acquisition and learning activities.

1   2   3   4

MELD is grounded in effective instruction for SELs that is based on the linguistic research and makes use of appropriate instructional tools.

1   2   3   4

MELD lessons address: ___ phonology ___ grammar ___ vocabulary development ___reading comprehension ___ written language development

| 1 | 2 | 3 | 4 |

MELD instruction results in tangible student work products that are displayed and can be used to assess progress toward meeting standards.

| 1 | 2 | 3 | 4 |

Students engage in reading, writing, and speaking activities on a daily basis.

| 1 | 2 | 3 | 4 |

Contrastive analysis is incorporated into daily instruction to support the development of academic language (oral language and writing skills).

| 1 | 2 | 3 | 4 |

Academic vocabulary development is incorporated into daily instruction through development and use of a personal thesaurus of conceptually coded words.

| 1 | 2 | 3 | 4 |

A classroom library of at least 200 books that reflect the culture, language, and experiences of the students in the classroom is invitingly displayed and utilized.

| 1 | 2 | 3 | 4 |

Oral language competence (i.e., storytelling, oration, and debate skills) is used as a scaffold to further the acquisition of school literacy.

| 1 | 2 | 3 | 4 |

The classroom environment is culturally relevant and responsive to students and includes cultural literature, artifacts, pictures of achievers, and so on.

| 1 | 2 | 3 | 4 |

REFLECT AND APPLY

Complete the CLRI Checklist, and rate your instruction and classroom environment. Where are you now in creating a culturally compatible classroom?

CHAPTER SIX

Conclusions, Challenges, and Connections

In conclusion, what we have attempted to do with this text is allay the notion that cultural variation does not matter in instruction. The old adage "I treat all my students the same no matter their background, ethnicity, culture or language" is problematic because students formed and shaped in varying cultural milieus are not the same. They bring important differences to the learning environment that must be considered in the developing of the curriculum, the instructional design, and in how the learning environment is structured. ELs and SELs bring cultural and linguistic variations to the classroom that do not match the cultural paradigm of traditional American schools and thus do not match teacher expectation, and their opportunity to learn at high levels is often compromised by deficit views relative to both their language and culture. They deserve better; they deserve, as all students do, access to rigorous learning opportunities in instructional environments that accept, affirm, and accommodate them as learners. It is our hope that this text will help teachers become the culturally competent educators our ELL and SEL students deserve.

TUNING PROTOCOL: POWERFUL PROFESSIONAL LEARNING TO ENHANCE ELL AND SEL ACHIEVEMENT

To understand and implement the work of this series, we advocate sustained, job-embedded professional learning that is grounded in the work of teacher teams. Reading this book can be a starting place for such learning, and the Tuning Protocol is a tool for self-reflection when analyzing student work samples for ALD.

Specifically, the Tuning Protocol is a powerful design for professional learning that is based on collaborative analysis of student work. Due to the fact that it takes focused professional development over time to change major instructional practices, we recommend that a recursive professional development sequence, like the Tuning Protocol, be used along with the book series. The Tuning Protocol, developed by the Coalition of Essential Schools (Blythe, Allen, & Powell, 1999), can be effective as a way to more deeply explore ALD strategies and approaches recommended throughout the book series. For example, a department or grade level may choose to analyze student work samples from ELLs and/or SELs that address paragraph structures from *Grammar and Syntax in Context* or to analyze the conversational skill of clarifying ideas from *Conversational Discourse in Context*. A full-cycle collaborative conversation of the Tuning Protocol for culturally responsive teaching is provided here.

THE TUNING PROTOCOL

(1) Presenter describes context of the work to be analyzed (e.g., student level, curriculum, or time allotted).

   Presenter determines focus question, which will be the lens by which the work will be analyzed.

(2) Group silently reviews work and asks clarifying question only (e.g., How long did it take?).

(3) Group takes notes on warm and cool feedback *regarding the focus question only.*

(4) Group shares warm and cool feedback.

(5) Presenter reflects on next steps for instruction.

(Adapted by Soto, 2012)

TUNING PROTOCOL FOR GROUP WORK

In Chapter 3, you read about the five laws of effective teaching for ELLs and SELs, and the second law which emphasizes connecting instruction to students' prior knowledge and experiences. One of the strategies highlighted is the use of advanced organizers. Advanced organizers are described as

> activities completed prior to learning or to introducing new material that help students anticipate, organize, and sometimes reorganize their thinking. They are designed to bridge the gap between what the learner already knows—prior knowledge—and what he or she needs to learn and to orient them to what it is they will be learning. The use of advance organizers has been shown, through research (Ruthkosky & Dwyer, 1996; Joyce, Weil, & Calhoun, 2003; Mayer, 2003), to improve levels of understanding and recall, particularly for culturally and linguistically diverse students. Advance organizers present information that can be used by ELL and SEL students to interpret new, incoming information. They may take different forms including clear teacher instructions, graphic organizers, or what are sometimes referred to as concept maps. The objective is to enhance students' ability to receive, store, and recall information and to provide them with clear orientation to the learning task.

Once the teacher has read the story *Stellaluna* to students, they can reread the text in small groups and complete the Reciprocal Teaching advanced organizer, where each student takes on a role (summarizer, questioner, predictor, and/or connector). The advanced organizers can then be analyzed using the Tuning Protocol, as follows:

(1) **Teacher describes the context of the work to the group**— "I used the Reciprocal Teaching advanced organizer after I read the story *Stellaluna* (the story of a bat who is separated from her mother and raised by birds) to students as a read aloud. In heterogeneous groups of four, I assigned each of my students a Reciprocal Teaching role (summarizer, questioner, predictor, and/or connector) and had them reread the text together in their small groups. My students are in the third grade, and I intentionally placed ELLs in groups with linguistic models."

(a) **Presenter determines focus question for analysis of student sample**—The teacher decides that as her colleagues analyze the Reciprocal Teaching advanced organizer from an ELL, she would like them to focus on how her ELL student can elaborate her written response connected to the summarizing role. The focus question then becomes, "How can I assist my ELL student with elaborating on her summary?"

(2) **Group reviews work and asks clarifying questions**—One colleague asked the clarifying question: "How did you first introduce the Reciprocal Teaching?" The teacher responds, "First, I introduced each of the four roles individually with the whole class using a familiar text. Then, I modeled each of the four roles using a think aloud and evidence from the familiar text. Last, I completed each of the roles on the advanced organizer so that students could see the response under the document reader."

 (a) **Group individually takes notes, highlighting warm and cool feedback**—For warm feedback, participants will analyze the student work sample for everything that was done well, from punctuation, to evidence, to penmanship. For cool (not cold) feedback, participants will analyze the student work sample according to the focus question only. Recall that the teacher presenter selected the focus question, so that she was in control of the type of cool feedback that she wished to receive. In this example, the teacher asked for the following cool feedback: "How can I assist my ELL student with elaborating on her summary?"

 (b) **Group shares warm and cool feedback**—One at a time, participants in the group share warm feedback first. It is helpful to use objective frames when providing feedback, such as "I noticed (*for observations*)" and "I wonder (*for questions*)." It is also important to begin with warm feedback as we all want to be viewed from an asset model first. A sample warm feedback statement might be: "*I noticed* that the student included three ideas for her summary." (Please note that if the Tuning Protocol is being used with a large group, the group facilitator will want to select a few warm and cool feedback statements.) Once the warm feedback has been shared, cool feedback statements can be provided. Recall that cool feedback is based on the focus question only. In this case, the teacher wanted cool feedback regarding the following question: "How can I assist my ELL student with elaborating on her summary?" A sample cool feedback statement might be: "She included three summary statements, but she was quite brief and did not include evidence from the text. *I wonder* if using a sentence frame that required evidence from the text would assist this ELL with elaboration?"

(3) **Presenter reflects on feedback provided**—After all of the warm and cool feedback has been provided, the teacher presenter reflects on her next steps from the group discussion of the student work sample on supporting ideas. A sample reflective statement might be: "My next step with having my students, especially this ELL, elaborate on her summary statement, is to include a sentence frame that requires evidence from the text for the response. I'm even thinking of typing the frame right into the advanced organizer."

We recognize that for many teachers, the ideas in this book and the book series will require time and practice. Both sustained professional development over time (which can include the Tuning Protocol) and instructional coaching can be helpful tools. It is also important for educators to remember to go slow to go fast, that is, to realize that the strategies and instructional approaches outlined will take time to approximate. In this manner, just as we honor the assets of our students, let's honor the assets of our teachers as excellent learners, who can take on new challenges with appropriate and sustained professional development over time.

ALD BOOK SERIES SUMMARY AND INTERSECTIONS ACROSS BOOK SERIES

As suggested earlier, the purpose of this four-book series is to assist educators in developing expertise in, and practical strategies for, addressing the key dimensions of academic language when working

ALD Dimension	Book Series Summary	Intersections Across Book Series
Conversational Discourse	Zwiers (2016) defines *conversational discourse* as the use of language for extended, back-and-forth, and purposeful communication among people. A key feature of conversational discourse is that it is used to create and clarify knowledge, not just transmit it. The essential skills of conversational discourse include the following: ● Conversing with a purpose ● Clarifying ideas ● Supporting ideas and finding evidence ● Evaluating evidence and reasoning ● Negotiating ideas Successful conversational discourse for ELLs and SELs requires a safe classroom culture and appropriate scaffolds for conversation.	● Conversational discourse necessarily connects to the development of *academic vocabulary* and to its written counterpart, academic writing across genres. ● It connects to *grammar and syntax in context* through the need to make and express meaning at the text, paragraph, and sentence levels. ● It connects to *culturally and linguistically responsive practices* by engaging students in cooperative practices and respectful listening to other points of view and backgrounds.
Academic Vocabulary	Calderón and Soto (2016) define *academic vocabulary* as a combination of words, phrases, sentences, and strategies to participate in class discussions, to show evidence of understanding and express complex concepts in texts, and to express oneself in academic writing. To enhance academic vocabulary for ELLs and SELs, teachers select words to specifically teach before, during, and after instruction. They select words and phrases that they believe ELLs and SELs need ● to know to comprehend the text. ● to discuss those concepts. ● to use in their writing later on.	● Academic vocabulary, according to Calderón, is the centerpiece of *conversational discourse.* ● It connects to *grammar and syntax in context* naturally in that vocabulary is also taught within context. The two dimensions mutually provide meaning for one another. ● It connects to *culturally and linguistically responsive practices* in making understandable the distinctions between some common misuses of words ("berry" instead of "very") and the standard English word association.

ALD Dimension	Book Series Summary	Intersections Across Book Series
Grammar and Syntax in Context	According to Soto, Freeman, & Freeman (2016), academic texts pose a particular challenge to ELLs and SELs because they contain technical vocabulary and grammatical structures that are lexically dense and abstract. These include long nominal groups, passives, and complex sentences. ELLs and SELs need carefully scaffolded instruction to write the academic genres, make the writing cohesive, and use appropriate grammatical structures.	• ELLs and SELs need to be engaged in academic discourse to develop their oral academic language. This provides the base for reading and writing academic texts. • ELLs and SELs also need to develop academic vocabulary, both content specific vocabulary and general academic vocabulary that they can use as they read and write the academic genres. • Teachers should use culturally and linguistically responsive practices that enable students to draw on their full linguistic repertoires.
Culturally and Linguistically Responsive Practices	LeMoine cites Gay (2000) in defining *culturally and linguistically responsive practices* as "ways of knowing, understanding, and representing various ethnic groups in teaching academic subjects, processes, and skills." Its primary features benefitting ELLs and SELs include the following: • Promoting cooperation, collaboration, reciprocity, and mutual responsibility for learning • Incorporating high-status, accurate cultural knowledge about different groups of students • Cultivating the cultural integrity, individual abilities, and academic success of diverse student groups Simply stated, it is meaningful learning embedded in language and culture.	• Culturally and linguistically responsive practices connect to the development of *academic vocabulary* by providing recognition for prior knowledge and acknowledging culture as part of linguistic development. • It connects to conversational discourse by prioritizing cooperative conversation procedures and minimizing confrontational discourse. • It connects to grammar and syntax in context by building on second language acquisition strategies and methods (such as SDAIE [Specially Designed Academic Instruction in English] and contrastive analysis).

with ELLs and SELs. In order to systemically address the needs of ELLs and SELs, we educators must share a common understanding of academic language development and the interconnectedness of its four dimensions.

The chart on pages 74–75 provides a summary of the ALD dimension as well as intersections across the book series. To truly create systemic change for ELLs and SELs in the area of ALD, there must be a deep understanding of each of the dimensions of ALD under study, as well as sustained professional development and instructional efforts to address each dimension, which will be addressed throughout the book series.

The chart allows us to better understand how ALD can and will support ELLs and SELS to make connections within new, rigorous standards and expectations. Meaningful and intentional planning around each ALD dimension will allow access for ELLs and SELs into content that might otherwise be inaccessible to them. Both in the next section and in the epilogue, you will learn how to use this series in professional development settings and how the book series connects to culturally and linguistically responsive practices.

ICLRT DESIGN PRINCIPLES CONNECTION TO CLRP

This text on CLRP in the ALD series makes connection with all of the ICLRT Design Principles as explained below:

DESIGN PRINCIPLE 1

Connecting and addressing the needs of both ELLs and SELs, both linguistically and culturally,

ELs and SELs both bring cultural and linguistic diversity to the classroom. They bring different cultural learning styles, cognitive styles, and ways of interacting and responding that do not match the traditional European-centered norms in American schools, and as a result, adjustments will be required in how learning environments are structured and instruction designed to accommodate and build on the cultural and linguistic strengths and differences they bring to the learning environment.

DESIGN PRINCIPLE 2

Assisting educators with identifying ways to use this book series (and additional ICLRT books) in professional development settings

The research suggests goal setting, along with collaboration, regular monitoring, and adjusting actions toward those goals, produces positive results. Thus, for teachers to become competent culturally conscious educators, who as Lindsey, Robins, and Terrell (2009) contend, see difference and understand the difference they make in how the learning environment should be structured, they must themselves be participants in learning communities that foster professional growth. Teachers must become researchers engaged in the dynamic process of knowledge building, collaboration, and critical inquiry toward the goal of increasing their knowledge and understanding of CLRP, teaching and lesson planning, student learning and achievement, effective instructional methodologies, and optimal instructional resources.

DESIGN PRINCIPLE 3

Addressing the underdeveloped domains of speaking and listening as areas that can be integrated across disciplines and components of ALD

CLRP acknowledges that all learning begins with the learner, what he or she brings to the learning community; his or her language, cultural experiences, learning styles, and strengths are "ground zero" for building new knowledge and understandings. If ELL and SEL students are to be successful in American educational institutions, they must become proficient in the literacies of its schools, thus the development of listening and speaking skills that support learning and facilitate access to core academic curricula are critical to their academic success. A curriculum that integrates listening and speaking enhances students' abilities to question, reflect, analyze, and synthesize information, drawing upon their prior knowledge and cultural experiences as they build new understandings and acquire new knowledge.

Design Principle 4

Integrating culturally responsive teaching as a vehicle for honoring both home and primary languages as well as cultural norms for learning

Culture is an all-encompassing phenomenon that determines who we are, how we live, and what we value and greatly influences how we learn. It cannot be separated from the learning environment, and teachers who attempt to stifle the influences of students' culture and language on learning, instead of incorporating them into the instructional design, have a recipe for disaster. No child can learn in contexts where who they are is ignored or all that is meaningful to them is demeaned. Unless students feel valued and affirmed as learners who have the capacity to achieve at the highest levels, and their cultural strengths are accommodated in instruction, learning simply will not occur.

Epilogue: The Vision

The vision for this book series began with the formation of the Institute for Culturally and Linguistically Responsive Teaching (ICLRT) at Whittier College, the creation of the ICLRT Design Principles which guide the institute, and the development of an ALD book series, which can assist educators with more deeply meeting the needs of their ELLs and SELs. ICLRT was formed in 2014, and the institute's mission is to, "promote relevant research and develop academic resources for ELLs and Standard English Learners (SELs) via linguistically and culturally responsive teaching practices" (ICLRT, n.d.). As such, ICLRT's purpose is to "provide research-based and practitioner-oriented professional development services, tools, and resources for K–12 systems and teacher education programs serving ELLs and SELs." Whittier College is a nationally designated Hispanic-Serving Institution, and ICLRT staff have been providing professional development on ELLs and SELs for more than 15 years, both across California and nationally.

The four books in this ALD series build upon the foundation of the ICLRT Design Principles:

(1) Connecting and addressing the needs of both ELLs and SELs, both linguistically and culturally

(2) Assisting educators with identifying ways to use this book series (and additional ICLRT books) in professional development settings

(3) Addressing the underdeveloped domains of speaking and listening as areas that can be integrated across disciplines and components of ALD

(4) Integrating culturally responsive teaching as a vehicle for honoring both home and primary languages as well as cultural norms for learning

ICLRT DESIGN PRINCIPLES

Here is a complete list of the ICLRT Design Principles. In parentheses are the books in this series that will address each principle.

(1) **ICLRT believes that the commonalities between ELL and SEL students are more extensive (and more vital to their learning) than the differences between the two groups.**

- ELL and SEL students are at the same end of the learning gap—they often score at the lowest levels on achievement tests. They also rank highly among high school dropouts (*Culture in Context*).
- The academic progress of ELL and SEL students may be hindered by barriers, such as poor identification practices and negative teacher attitudes towards their languages and cultures (*Culture in Context*).
- ELL and SEL students both need specific instructional attention to the development of academic language development (*Grammar and Syntax in Context, Conversational Discourse in Context, Vocabulary in Context*).

(2) **ICLRT believes that ongoing, targeted professional development is the key to redirecting teacher attitudes toward ELL and SEL student groups.**

- Teacher knowledge about the histories and cultures of ELL and SEL students can be addressed through professional development and professional learning communities (*Culture in Context*).
- Teachers will become aware of the origins of nonstandard language usage (*Culture in Context*).
- Teachers can become aware of and comfortable with using diverse texts and productive group work to enhance students' sense of belonging (*Conversational Discourse in Context*).
- The ICLRT Academic Language Certification process will provide local demonstration models of appropriate practices and attitudes (*Conversational Discourse in Context*).

(3) **ICLRT believes that ELL and SEL students need to have ongoing, progressive opportunities for listening and speaking throughout their school experiences.**

- The typical ELD sequence of curriculum and courses do not substantially address ELL and SEL student needs for language development (*Conversational Discourse*, and *Vocabulary in Context*).
- The ICLRT student shadowing protocol and student shadowing app can provide both quantitative and qualitative information about student speaking and listening (*Conversational Discourse in Context*).
- The ICLRT lesson plan design incorporates appropriate speaking and listening development, integrated with reading, writing, and/or content area learning (*Conversational Discourse in Context*).
- Strategies for active listening and academic oral language are embedded in ICLRT's ALD professional development series (*Conversational Discourse in Context*).

(4) **ICLRT believes that its blending of culturally responsive pedagogy (CRP) with ALD will provide teachers of ELL and SEL students with powerful learning tools and strategies.**

- The six characteristics of CRP (Gay, 2000), along with the procedure of contrastive analysis, heighten the already strong effects of solid ALD instruction (*Grammar and Syntax in Context*).
- The storytelling aspects of CRP fit well with the oral language traditions of ELLs, and can be used as a foundational tool for both groups to affirm their rich histories (*Culture in Context*).
- Both groups need specific instruction in the four essential components of ALD, including SDAIE strategies (*Grammar and Syntax in Context*, *Conversational Discourse in Context*, and *Vocabulary in Context*).
- The inclusion of CRP and ALD within the ICLRT lesson planning tool makes their use seamless instead of disparate for each group (*Culture in Context*).

Sources: Gay (2000); LeMoine, 1999; Soto-Hinman & Hetzel (2009).

Additional ICLRT Professional Development Resources

This ALD book series is one of the research-based resources developed by ICLRT to assist K–12 systems in serving ELLs and SELs. Other ICLRT resources include the following Corwin texts: *The Literacy Gaps: Building Bridges for ELLs and SELs* (Soto-Hinman & Hetzel, 2009); *ELL Shadowing as a Catalyst for Change* (Soto, 2012); and *Moving From Spoken to Written Language With ELLs* (Soto, 2014). Together, the three books, and their respective professional development modules (available via ICLRT and Corwin), tell a story of how to systemically close achievement gaps with ELLs and SELs by increasing their academic oral language production in academic areas. Specifically, each ICLRT book in the series addresses ALD in the following ways.

- *The Literacy Gaps: Building Bridges for ELLs and SELs* (Soto-Hinman & Hetzel, 2009)—This book is a primer for meeting the literacy needs of ELLs and SELs. Additionally, the linguistic and achievement needs of ELLs and SELs are linked and specific ALD strategies are outlined to comprehensively and coherently meet the needs of both groups of students.
- *ELL Shadowing as a Catalyst for Change* (Soto, 2012)—This book is a way to create urgency around meeting the academic oral language needs of ELLs. Educators shadow an ELL student, guided by the ELL shadowing protocol, which allows them to monitor and collect academic oral language and active listening data. The ethnographic project allows educators to experience a day in the life of an ELL.
- *Moving From Spoken to Written Language With ELLs* (Soto, 2014)—This book assists educators in leveraging spoken language into written language. Specific strategies, such as Think-Pair-Share, the Frayer model, and Reciprocal Teaching, are used to scaffold the writing process, and the Curriculum Cycle (Gibbons, 2002) is recommended as a framework for teaching writing.

Please note that professional development modules for each of the texts listed above are also available through ICLRT. For more information, please go to www.whittier.edu/ICLRT.

The ALD book series can be used either after or alongside of *The Literacy Gaps: Building Bridges for ELLs and SELs* (Soto-Hinman & Hetzel, 2009); *ELL Shadowing as a Catalyst for Change* (Soto, 2012); and *Moving From Spoken to Written Language With ELLs* (Soto, 2014) as each book introduces and addresses the importance of ALD for ELLs and SELs. The ALD book series also takes each ALD component deeper by presenting specific research and strategies that will benefit ELLs and SELs in the classroom.

References

Academic Language Development Network. (n.d.). Retrieved from http://aldnetwork.org/

Bailey, C. T., & Boykin, A. W. (2001). The role of task variability and home contextual factors in the academic performance and task motivation of African American elementary school children. *Journal of Negro Education, 70*(1/2), 84–95.

Baldwin, J. (1979, July 29). If Black English isn't a language, then tell me, what is? *The New York Times.* Retrieved from http://www.nytimes.com

Blythe, T., Allen, D., & Powell, B. S. (1999). *Looking together at student work.* New York: College Teachers Press.

Boykin, W. (1997, October). Cultural factors in school-relevant cognitive functioning. Paper presented at the Congressional Black Caucus Education Forum, Washington, DC.

Boykin, W. A. (2001). The challenges of cultural socialization in the schooling of African American elementary school children: Exposing the hidden curriculum. In W. H. Watkins, J. H. Lewis, & V. Chou (Eds.), *Race and education: The roles of history and society in educating African American students* (pp. 190–199). Needham Heights, MA: Allyn & Bacon.

Boykin, A. W., & Cunningham, R. T. (2001). The effects of movement expressiveness in story content and learning context on the analogical reasoning performance of African American children. *Journal of Negro Education, 70*(1–2), 72–83.

Boykin, A. W., Lilja, A., & Tyler, K. M. (2004). The influence of communal vs. individual learning context on the academic performance in social studies of grades 4–5 African Americans. *Learning Environment Research 7*, 227–244.

Calderón, M., & Soto, I. (2016). *Academic English mastery: Vocabulary in context.* Thousand Oaks, CA: Corwin.

Cole, L. (1991). *Trainer's handbook for dual linguistic instruction of African American children.* Unpublished manuscript.

Cornell Center for Teaching Excellence. (n.d.). *Assessing student learning: What do students already know?* Retrieved from http://www.cte.cornell.edu

Cummins, J. (2000). *Language, power and pedagogy: Bilingual children in the crossfire.* Cleveland, OH: Multilingual Matters.

Cummins, J. (2001). *Negotiating identities: Education for empowerment in a diverse society* (2nd ed.). Ontario, CA: California Association for Bilingual Education.

Darling-Hammond, L. (2015, April). Proven educational programs. Keynote address. Twenty-ninth annual National Council on Educating Black Children meeting. Indianapolis, IN.

Darling-Hammond, L. (1997). *The right to learn: A blueprint for creating schools that work.* San Francisco, CA: Jossey-Bass.

Delpit, L. (2006). *Other people's children: Cultural conflict in the classroom.* New York: Norton.

Delpit, L., & Dowdy, J. (Eds.). (2002). *The skin we speak: Thoughts on language and culture in the classroom.* New York: The New Press.

Gay, G. (2000). *Culturally responsive teaching: Theory, research, & practice.* New York: Teachers College Press.

Gibbons, P. (2002). *Scaffolding language, scaffolding learning: Teaching second language learners in the mainstream classroom.* Portsmouth, NH: Heinemann.

Harris, V. (1995). Using African American literature in the classroom. In V. Gadsden & D. Wagner (Eds.), *Literacy among African-American youth.* New Jersey: Hampton Press.

Hilliard, A. G. (1992). Behavioral style, culture, and teaching and learning. *Journal of Negro Education 61,* 370–377.

Hollins, E., & Oliver, E. (1999). *Pathways to success in school: Culturally responsive teaching.* Mahwah, NJ: Lawrence Erlbaum.

Hurley, E. A. (1999). *The interaction of culture with math achievement and group processes among African American and European American students.* Paper presented at the annual meeting of the American Educational Research Association (AERA), New Orleans, LA.

Hurley, E. A., Boykin, A. W., & Allen, B. A. (2005). Communal versus individual learning of a math-estimation task: African American children and the culture of learning contexts *The Journal of Psychology, 139*(6), 513–527.

Institute for Culturally and Linguistically Responsive Teaching (ICLRT). (n.d.). Retrieved from http://www.whittier.edu/ICLRT

Institute for Learning (IFL). (n.d.). *Principles of learning.* An outreach of the University of Pittsburgh's Learning Research and Development Center (LRDC). Retrieved from http://www.ifl,pitt.edu

Irvine, J., & Armento, B. (2001). Culturally responsive teaching, lesson planning for elementary and middle grades. New York: McGraw-Hill.

Joyce, B., Weil, M., & Calhoun, E. (2003). *Models of teaching* (7th ed.). Englewood Cliffs, NJ: Prentice Hall.

Keefe, J.W. (1979). Learning style: An overview. In *Student learning styles: Diagnosing and prescribing programs* (pp. 1–17). Reston, VA: National Association of Secondary School Principals.

Krashen, S. (2004). *The power of reading.* Portsmouth, NH: Heinemann.

Labov, W. (1972, June). Academic ignorance and Black intelligence. *The Atlantic Monthly Digital Edition.* Retrieved from http://www.the atlantic.com

Ladson-Billings, G. (2005). The evolving role of critical race theory in educational scholarship. *Race, Ethnicity & Education*, 8(1), 115–119.

Ladson-Billings, G. (2009). *The dreamkeepers: Successful teachers of African American children* (2nd ed.). San Francisco, CA: Jossey-Bass.

Leap, W. (1993). *American Indian English.* Salt Lake City: University of Utah Press.

LeMoine, N. (2001). Language variation and literacy acquisition in African American students. In J. Harris, A. Kamhi, & K. Pollock (Eds.), *Literacy in African American communities* (pp. 169–194). Mahwah, NJ: Lawrence Erlbaum.

LeMoine, N. R. (2003). *The impact of linguistic knowledge of African American language/Ebonics on teacher attitude toward African American language and the students who speak AAL/Ebonics.* Doctoral dissertation, University of Southern California, Los Angeles. UMI Dissertation Abstract database, 31-3935.

LeMoine, N., & Los Angeles Unified School District. (1999). *English for your success: A language development program for African American students.* New Jersey: Peoples Publishing Group.

Lindsey, R., Robins, K., & Terrell, R. (2009) *Cultural proficiency: A manual for school leaders* (3rd ed.). Thousand Oaks, CA: Corwin.

Marri, A. (2005). *Building a framework for classroom-based multicultural democratic education: Learning from three skilled teachers.* Teachers College Record, 107, 1036-1059.

Mayer, R. (2003). *Learning and instruction.* New Jersey: Pearson.

McQuillan, J., & Krashen, S. (2008). Commentary: Can free reading take you all the way? A response to Cobb (2007). *Language & Technology*, *12*(1), 104–108.

Migration Policy Institute Tabulation of Data From the United Nations, Department of Economic and Social Affairs. (2013). Trends in international migrant stock: Migrants by origin and destination, 2013 revision (United Nations database, POP/DB/MIG/Stock/Rev.2013). Retrieved from http://esa.un.org/unmigration/TIMSO2013/migrant stocks2013.htm

Nobles, W. W. (2015). Lecture on the western grand narrative and major impact on psychology. Retrieved from http://instagram.com/p/yQ1 DHtRlDd/

Obama, B. (2009, March 10). *Remarks of the president to the United States Hispanic Chamber of Commerce*. The White House, Washington, DC. Retrieved from http://www.whitehouse.gov

Ogbu, J. (Ed.). (2008). *Minority status, oppositional culture, and schooling*. New York: Rutledge.

O'Neil, J. (1990). Making sense of style. *Educational Leadership, 42*, 4–9.

Owocki, G., & Goodman, Y. (2002). *Kidwatching: Documenting children's literacy*. Portsmouth, NH: Heinemann.

Palmer, P. J. (2007). *The courage to teach: Exploring the inner landscape of a teacher's life*. San Francisco, CA: Jossey-Bass.

Pressley, M., & Allington, R. (2014). Reading instruction that works: The case for balanced teaching (4th ed.). New York: Guildford.

Pritchard, A. (2014). *Ways of learning: Learning theories and learning styles in the classroom* (3rd ed.). New York: Routledge.

Ruthkosky, K. O., & Dwyer, F. M. (1996). The effect of adding visualization and rehearsal strategies to advance organizers in facilitating long-term retention. *International Journal of Instructional Media, 23*(1), 31–40.

Soto, I. (2012). *ELL shadowing as a catalyst for change*. Thousand Oaks, CA: Corwin.

Soto, I. (2014). *From spoken to written language with ELLs*. Thousand Oaks, CA: Corwin.

Soto, I., Freeman, D., & Freeman, Y. (2016). *Academic English mastery: Grammar and syntax in context*. Thousand Oaks, CA: Corwin.

Soto-Hinman, I., & Hetzel, J. (2009). *The literacy gaps: Building bridges for ELLs and SELs*. Thousand Oaks, CA: Corwin.

Street, B. (1995). *Social literacies; Critical approaches to literacy in development, ethnography and education*. Essex, UK: Longman.

Tauber, R. (1997). *Self-fulfilling prophecy, a practical guide to its use in education*. Westport, CT: Praeger

Taylor, H. (1991). *Standard English, Black English and Bidialectalism: A controversy*. New York: Peter Lang.

Valenzuela, A. (1999). *Subtractive schooling: US Mexican youth and the politics of caring*. Albany: State University of New York Press.

Villegas, A., & Lucas, T. (2002). Preparing culturally responsive teachers: Rethinking the curriculum, *Journal of Teacher Education, 53*. doi: 10.1177/ 0022487102053001003

Vygotsky, L. S. (1978). *Mind in society: The development of higher psychological processes*. Cambridge, MA: Harvard University Press.

WIDA Consortium. (2014). *Focus on American Indian English language learners*. WCER University of Wisconsin–Madison. Retrieved from http://www.wida.us

Wong-Fillmore, L. (2013). Defining academic language. *Education Week.* Retrieved from http://www.edweek.org/ew/articles/2013/10/30/10cc-academiclanguage.h33.html

Zwiers, J. (2016). *Academic English mastery: Conversational skills in context.* Thousand Oaks, CA: Corwin.

Index

IS YOUR ACADEMIC LANGUAGE MASTERY LIBRARY COMPLETE?

Academic Language Mastery: Conversational Discourse in Context
Jeff Zwiers and Ivannia Soto

Here, Jeff Zwiers reveals the power of academic conversation in helping students develop language, clarify concepts, comprehend complex texts, and fortify thinking and relational skills. With this book as your road map, you'll learn how to

- Foster the skills and language students must develop for productive interactions
- Implement strategies for scaffolding conversations between students
- Formatively assess students' oral language development

Academic Language Mastery: Grammar and Syntax in Context
David E. Freeman, Yvonne S. Freeman, and Ivannia Soto

David and Yvonne Freeman shatter the myth that academic language is all about vocabulary, revealing how grammar and syntax inform ELLs' and SELs' grasp of challenging text. Inside you'll find research-backed advice on how to

- Teach grammar in the context of students' speech and writing
- Use strategies such as sentence frames, passives, combining simple sentences into more complex sentences, and nominalization to create more complex noun phrases
- Assess academic language development through a four-step process

Academic Language Mastery: Vocabulary in Context
Margarita Calderón and Ivannia Soto

Vocabulary instruction is not an end in itself. Instead, academic words are best taught as tools for completing and constructing more complex messages. Look to renowned author Margarita Calderón for expert guidelines on how to

- Teach high-frequency academic words and discipline-specific vocabulary across content areas
- Utilize strategies for teaching academic vocabulary, moving students from Tier 1 to Tiers 2 and 3 words and selecting appropriate words to teach
- Assess vocabulary development as you go

A SAGE Publishing Company

Helping educators make the greatest impact

CORWIN HAS ONE MISSION: to enhance education through intentional professional learning.

We build long-term relationships with our authors, educators, clients, and associations who partner with us to develop and continuously improve the best evidence-based practices that establish and support lifelong learning.

Solutions you want. Experts you trust. Results you need.